Awakening the Kind Heart

KATHLEEN MCDONALD
(Sangye Khandro)

AWAKENING

the *Kind Heart*

HOW TO
MEDITATE ON
COMPASSION

WISDOM PUBLICATIONS • BOSTON

Wisdom Publications
199 Elm Street
Somerville MA 02144 USA
www.wisdompubs.org

Library of Congress Cataloging-in-Publication Data
McDonald, Kathleen, 1952–
 Awakening the kind heart : how to meditate on compassion / Kathleen McDonald (Sangye Khadro).
    p. cm.
 Includes bibliographical references.
 ISBN 0-86171-695-7 (pbk. : alk. paper)
 1. Meditation—Buddhism. 2. Compassion—Religious aspects—Buddhism. 3. Spiritual life—Buddhism. I. Title.
 BQ5612.M325 2010
 294.3'4435—dc22

                                        2010007993

14 13 12 11 10
5 4 3 2 1

Drawings of Chenrezig and Maitreya by Robert Beer. Cover design by Phil Pascuzzo. Interior design by LC. Set in Bembo 11/15.5.

Wisdom Publications' books are printed on acid-free paper and meet the guidelines for permanence and durability of the Production Guidelines for Book Longevity of the Council on Library Resources.

Printed in the United States of America.

This book was produced with environmental mindfulness. We have elected to print this title on 30% PCW recycled paper. As a result, we have saved the following resources: 17 trees, 5 million BTUs of energy, 1,617 lbs. of greenhouse gases, 7,795 gallons of water, and 472 lbs. of solid waste. For more information, please visit our website, www.wisdompubs.org. This paper is also FSC certified. For more information, please visit www.fscus.org.

Table of Contents

Publisher's Acknowledgment

The publisher gratefully acknowledges the generous help of the Hershey Family Foundation in sponsoring the publication of this book.

Preface

Whether one believes in a religion or not, and whether one believes in rebirth or not, there isn't anyone who doesn't appreciate kindness and compassion.
—His Holiness the Dalai Lama[1]

*E*veryone appreciates kindness. A smile, a few friendly words, a show of concern when we're troubled or feeling unwell, an offer of help—gestures of kindness like these brighten our day and ease whatever sadness we may feel in our hearts. Feeling that "someone cares about me" fulfills a very deep need that we all have. And just as we appreciate other people being kind to us, others appreciate it when we are kind to them. That is why it is important to learn to be kind, because it will help make our relationships and interactions with others more satisfying and more problem-free.

But it's not always easy to be kind. Sometimes our hearts are filled with anger or hatred, jealousy, or pride, and being kind is the last thing we feel like doing. Or we get so caught up in our work and responsibilities that we find no time to think of others and their needs, no time to be kind and gentle. However, these problems can be remedied. The Buddhist tradition offers a wealth of methods that can be used to overcome whatever prevents us from being kind, such as anger or selfishness, and to practice kindness more in our daily life. As His Holiness the Dalai Lama says, "My religion is kindness."

Some of these methods are explored and explained in this book—in a way that will allow you to practice them in your daily life. Two main traditions of practicing kind-heartedness are introduced here. The four immeasurable thoughts—love, compassion, joy, and equanimity—are essential practices in all traditions of Buddhism. In section one, one chapter is devoted to each of these, with meditations on love and compassion included in separate chapters and meditations on joy and equanimity at the end of their respective chapters to help you actualize these four profound thoughts in your day-to-day life.

The second type of practice explored in this book, thought transformation (*lojong* in Tibetan), is a powerful method of practice in the Indo-Tibetan tradition that is becoming better known in the West. We will explore it in section two using *The Eight Verses of Thought Transformation*, composed by the eleventh-century Tibetan meditation master Geshe Langri Tangpa.[2] The *Eight Verses* is a beautiful little text, easily memorized, that offers us precious gems of wisdom on how to transform difficult situations into opportunities for spiritual growth—to transform pain into joy and lightness.

The explanations of these compassion teachings are not scholarly commentaries. Rather, I am simply sharing some things I have learned in my studies of Buddhism, as well as in my attempts to practice these teachings in my life. I have found these teachings very helpful, and I hope and expect others will too.

Awakening the Kind Heart was originally published by Amitabha Buddhist Centre, Singapore, in 1995, as a small booklet for free distribution. For this present edition, I revised and expanded the original material and added a number of meditations.

This book has come about through the kindness of many people. I would first of all like to thank from the depths of my heart my teachers, especially His Holiness the Dalai Lama, Lama Thubten Yeshe, Lama Thubten Zopa Rinpoche, Geshe Ngawang Dhargyey, Geshe Jampa Tegchog, Ribur Rinpoche, and the many other precious masters from whom I learned about kindness and compassion, not only from their teachings but from their perfect, living example. I also give my heartfelt thanks to Venerables Drolkar, Dekyong, and Sarah Tenzin Yiwong, and to Doris Low, Paul Ferguson, and Don Brown for their help with the original booklet, and to freelance editor Barry Boyce and Josh Bartok of Wisdom Publications for their invaluable editing assistance in this new edition. Many thanks as well to Snow Lion Publications for permission to use the quotations of His Holiness the Dalai Lama. Last but not least, I extend my deepest gratitude to my late parents, David and June McDonald, my first teachers of loving-kindness.

May this work help to bring peace and happiness to the minds and lives of all beings everywhere.

The Metta Sutta:
The Buddha's Words on Loving-Kindness

This is what should be done
By one who is skilled in goodness
And who knows the path of peace:
Let them be able and upright,
Straightforward and gentle in speech.
Humble and not conceited,
Contented and easily satisfied.
Unburdened with duties and frugal in their ways,
Peaceful and calm, and wise and skillful,
Not proud and demanding in nature.
Let them not do the slightest thing
That the wise would later reprove.
Wishing: In gladness and in safety,
May all beings be at ease.
Whatever living beings there may be,
Whether they are weak or strong, omitting none,
The great or the mighty, medium, short, or small,
The seen and the unseen,
Those living near and far away,
Those born and to-be-born,
May all beings be at ease!

Let none deceive another,
Or despise any being in any state.
Let none through anger or ill-will
Wish harm upon another.
Even as a mother protects with her life
Her child, her only child,
So with a boundless heart
Should one cherish all living beings:
Radiating kindness over the entire world
Spreading upward to the skies,
And downward to the depths;
Outward and unbounded,
Freed from hatred and ill-will.
Whether standing or walking, seated or lying down,
Free from drowsiness,
One should sustain this recollection.
This is said to be the sublime abiding.
By not holding to fixed views,
The pure-hearted one, having clarity of vision,
Being freed from all sense desires,
Is not born again into this world.

Section
ONE

1

It's Time to Change Your Mind

The Buddha was once an ordinary person like us. He had problems in relationships and problems within himself. He was disturbed by negative thoughts and emotions. Knowing that others experienced the same difficulties, he embarked on a spiritual journey to find an end to suffering. His search led him to the attainment of enlightenment and to his proclamation of the Four Noble Truths: there is suffering, it has a cause, it can be ended, and there is a path we can follow that leads to the end of suffering.

Paradoxically, to understand the state of enlightenment the Buddha attained, you have to be enlightened yourself. But we can get an idea of it. It's a state of mind in which all negative, harmful qualities—anger, hatred, greed, pride, ignorance, and so forth—have been eliminated. Conversely, all positive, beneficial qualities—universal compassion and love, generosity, patience, and wisdom—have been perfected. Someone who has attained enlightenment is free of all problems and suffering such as pain, sickness, death, fear, sadness, loneliness, and so forth, and is capable of helping all other beings to become free and to attain enlightenment. When we say we want to be happy, this is what we all are truly searching for.

The word *buddha* refers to *anyone* who attains the state of enlightenment. There are many who have already become buddhas, and in fact *all* of us have the potential to become buddhas. This potential—known as buddha nature—is always within us, a natural part of our mind. Our mind's nature is clear and pure, like a cloudless sky or pure spring water, and is only temporarily polluted by obscurations such as negative emotions. These can be eliminated, allowing the true, pure nature of our mind to be revealed, which is compassion itself. A truly kind heart already exists in each and every one of us. It's just a matter of learning how to bring it out and expand it so that we can feel it more often, for more people and more beings—and eventually for all living beings.

The Mind Is the Source of All

To appreciate the path that reveals the pure, compassionate nature of our mind, it's helpful to explore what we mean by *mind* in Buddhism. Every being is endowed with a mind or consciousness, a continuously flowing, ever-changing stream of experiences including thoughts, emotions, sensory perceptions, memories, dreams, and so on and so on. Our mind is not physical—a collection of cells and atoms—but a completely non-physical kind of energy. It's not the brain, the nervous system, or any part of the body, but it does interact with and affect the brain and the body. We could say our body is like the hardware of a computer and our mind is like the software.

The Buddha expressed the importance of the mind in this famous verse from one of the most concise summaries of the Buddhadharma, a collection of verses called the *Dhammapada*:

> Mind is the forerunner of all states;
> Mind is chief, mind-made are they.
> If one speaks or acts with an impure mind, suffering follows,
> Like the wheel that follows the cart-pulling ox.

> Mind is the forerunner of all states;
> Mind is chief, mind-made are they.
> If one speaks or acts with a pure mind, happiness follows,
> Like one's shadow that never leaves.

In other words, mind creates our experiences, unhappy and happy. Unhappiness and problems are the result of "impure" or negative states of mind (such as anger, greed, and jealousy) as well as the actions they lead to, whereas happiness comes from "pure" or positive states of mind (such as compassion, love, and patience) and actions motivated by these. This understanding is not exclusive to Buddhism, but is also found in many other religions, spiritual traditions, and systems of philosophy.

Our mind is thus the source of suffering and peace. When the mind is controlled by delusions and karma, we suffer and circle in the never-ending trap of cyclic existence known as samsara. When we free the mind from negative states and develop positive states, we become free from suffering and experience the peace and happiness of liberation and enlightenment. It's just a question of changing our mind. And this process of changing our mind is one of the distinguishing marks of Buddhism: it gives us a variety of practices that enable us to deeply influence the direction of our mind and the behavior that results.

Changing Your Mind

We can transform our mind from negative to positive, miserable to peaceful, because our mind is impermanent, ever-changing. It is never the same from one moment to the next. Every moment brings new thoughts, feelings, and experiences, each of which lasts but a moment. Disappearing, each thought gives rise to the next. Since our mind changes naturally anyway, it is also possible for us to consciously change it. This is important to recognize.

You might think, "I'm just an angry person. This is my nature and I cannot change," or "I've always been depressed and always will be depressed. I'll never be happy." This cannot possibly be correct! If you look carefully at your mind and your experiences, you'll notice moments when you are not angry or depressed, and moments when you are loving or happy. If you *think* you can't change, you won't even try, but if you believe that transformation is possible, you will put your energy into it, and achieve it. Definitely.

I say this with great confidence, but not because I have been told to think this way. Rather, long experience has taught me that the mind can be changed for the better. When I was young, I was a very unhappy person. Although my external situation was quite good—I had a comfortable home, caring parents, plenty to eat, a good education—I was troubled and confused. Looking back now, I recognize that my mind was flooded with negative thoughts and emotions. I was often selfish, greedy, depressed, angry, and critical. And I had trouble getting along with people. I did not want to be like that, though. I wanted to be kind and happy, but I had no idea how to change.

In my teens I learned about Buddhism and other Eastern spiritual traditions through reading books and felt strongly attracted. Eventually I decided to travel to India, where many of these traditions have their roots. At the age of 21, I found myself in Dharamsala, in the foothills of the Himalayas, learning Buddhism from Tibetan lamas. One of the things that attracted me to Buddhism was its marvellous explanation of the mind and its potential for pure happiness and peace, as well as the fact that it presented a step-by-step method for how to achieve this. After working with these teachings for the last 35 years, I know that they work. It's not that my anger and selfishness have completely disappeared. They still arise. But they arise much less frequently than before, and more positive thoughts and feelings arise in their place. I know for sure that my basic nature is pure and that a kind heart can always be awakened in any moment.

If you're still skeptical about the changeability of the mind, try this experiment: Close your eyes and sit quietly for a few minutes. Let your body relax, and let your mind settle down in the present moment, right where you are. Just pay attention to your inner world, to what is happening in your mind. Let the thoughts, perceptions, feelings, and memories come and go. Don't try to stop them. Don't get caught up in them. Observe them as you would observe cars and pedestrians passing by in a street. Can you see how they change? Is there any experience that is permanent, frozen, always present in your mind, every single moment?

The transitory nature of our mind explains the confusing experience we sometimes have of opposing mental states: one moment we are happy, another moment sad; one moment steady with confidence, another moment shaky with doubt or fear; one moment full of love for a friend, another moment angry, seeing her as an enemy. This situation is normal and understandable considering the mind's impermanent nature, and the fact that our mind is not enlightened, and thus not free from disturbing, negative emotions. But, if we understand the changeability of the mind, we know that these negative mental states are not permanent, existing eternally. They can be completely eliminated, leaving our mind in its pure, natural state.

In the Buddhist teachings, we say the mind is like the sky—clear, vast, unimpeded. Disturbing thoughts and emotions are like clouds that pass through the sky. Clouds are transitory: when the right conditions are present, they appear, but they quickly change and disappear. Similarly, due to conditions, thoughts and emotions appear in our mind but they are momentary and soon disappear. Also, like clouds, thoughts and emotions are not solid and cannot harm us, so we need not be afraid of them. Although certain emotions can be "destructive," this happens only when we don't know how to manage them and to transform our mind. They have no power in and of themselves to harm us.

Working on our mind to bring about a positive transformation is the essence of Buddhism, and the reason we do this inner work is to increase happiness and decrease suffering—both for ourselves and for others. The real purpose of Buddhist meditation is not simply to calm ourselves, but rather to transform the mind. The meaning of the Tibetan word for meditation, *gom*, is "to familiarize." Meditation is making our mind more familiar with positive thoughts and emotions, and less familiar with negative ones. What we are most familiar with, or habituated to, is what arises most easily and frequently in our minds. If we have the habit of being critical, for example, always seeing faults in others, then critical thoughts will arise in us again and again, spontaneously, effortlessly. On the other hand, if we develop the habit of seeing the good in others and forgiving them for their mistakes, kind and forgiving thoughts will arise naturally in our minds.

Some people are born with an abundance of wholesome qualities. They are kind, peaceful, respectful, considerate of others, and enjoy doing positive deeds. The Buddhist explanation is that they made themselves familiar with these qualities in previous lives. Those of us who are lacking in these qualities did not do enough work in the past. In fact, we all *do* have these qualities. It's just that in some of us they are less developed due to lack of practice in previous lives. Buddhist practice is like learning to play the piano. The more you do it, the better you become. The more we practice being kind and helpful, the more these qualities will arise naturally and spontaneously.

Antidotes to Disturbing Thoughts and Emotions

While working on transforming our mind, we will inevitably face negative thoughts and emotions. Simply deciding to be more positive won't make all our negativities instantly go away. They may arise while we are meditating or during our daily life. In fact, in the process of working on our mind, we may notice negative thoughts and emotions we had not seen before. This can make us depressed, thinking we are hopeless and getting worse rather than better. We might even think that meditation is the cause of it, and that we should stop meditating. This would be like throwing away the medicine that can heal us just because we're unaccustomed to its taste.

Meditation does not cause more thoughts to come up in our mind. It simply makes us aware of how many thoughts there are, all of the time. The disturbing thoughts and feelings you notice have always been part of your mind, but you just didn't recognize them. Meditation naturally makes us more sensitive, more aware. When you enter the path of meditation, you need to be careful. Don't become discouraged. Think instead that you are fortunate to be able to recognize your mind as it is, so that you can work on it. Negative emotions do not simply go away by themselves; we need to counteract them with positive mental states. We will explore remedies to specific emotions such as anger and jealousy later in the book, but it will help to begin by going over a few general remedies we can use when disturbing thoughts and emotions appear in our mind.

BE MINDFUL OR SELF-AWARE.

This means paying attention to your mind and learning to recognize negative thoughts when they arise. True mindfulness, though, is more than simply being aware of thoughts; it also involves doing something to counteract the harmful ones. It's like a security guard in a bank, who doesn't just observe what is going on but looks out for potential trouble and puts a stop to it. In some cases, just noticing a negative thought with mindfulness is enough. You can then let it go. But you may not always be able to do this, especially if the thought is strong or habitual, so you may need to apply other antidotes.

It is important to understand that *you have a choice*. Whenever a negative thought or emotion arises in your mind, you do not have to go along with it. There are other things you can do. Habit makes it so easy to get caught up in a negative thought or emotion. Saying "no" to it is more difficult because that habit is less prevalent, but you can develop it.

REFLECT ON THE NATURE OF THE MIND.

As we discussed above, think of the mind as the vast, clear sky, and thoughts as clouds that appear, pass through, and disappear. They are transitory, not permanent aspects of your mind. You can also think of them as dreams (because they exist only in your own mind), rainbows (they appear due to conditions, and disappear when conditions change), mirages, or waves that rise and fall in the sea.

Recalling impermanence grounds us. It can help us calm down when our mind is overly emotional with happiness, anxiety, anger, and so on. There is a story I love from the Zen tradition. A man went to see a Zen master, very upset. He told the master of a major crisis happening in his life. The master listened calmly, then said, "It will go away."

After some time, the man again visited the Zen master, this time happily excited. He said, "Do you remember that problem I told you about last time? Well, now it's gone!"

The master calmly replied, "It will come back."

DE-IDENTIFY WITH THOUGHTS AND EMOTIONS.

We have the tendency to identify with whatever arises in our mind: "*I* am angry," or "*I* am depressed." This reinforces the negative thoughts and feelings, making it harder to let them go. It can also lead to guilt, self-criticalness, and self-hatred. In reality we are *not* our thoughts and emotions. As we have seen, they are merely momentary mental states, non-physical phenomena that arise and disappear, but it's easy to forget that. To counteract the tendency to identify with our emotions, we can say to ourselves, "Anger is in my mind" or "Depression is in my mind" instead of "I am angry/depressed." This gives us space and objectivity. It disempowers the emotion, enabling it to pass more quickly.

What a wonderful, liberating discovery! "I am not my anger, my depression, pride, selfish attachment; I am not my self-destructive tendencies; I am not my hurtful behavior to others. These are mere phenomena that pass through me, but not who I really am, so I don't have to identify with them." At first you may find it hard to believe, because you have been identifying with these thoughts and feelings for so long. But if you repeat this idea to yourself, every day, again and again, slowly it will sink in. Eventually, it will become your reality.

BE NON-JUDGMENTAL.

This remedy follows on from the previous two. Since negative thoughts and emotions are impermanent and not who we are, it's incorrect to judge ourselves for having them. We are not bad or negative. We are simply beings with delusions in our mind, because we have not yet attained enlightenment. It's not our fault. Judging and hating ourselves does not solve the problem of disturbing mental states. It just makes things worse, heaping more misery on top of what is already there. See if you can recognize the power of non-judgment, and if you notice self-criticalness happening, replace it with kindness and forgiveness for yourself.

THINK OF OTHERS WHO HAVE SIMILAR PROBLEMS.

When we are experiencing an emotional problem, we tend to get obsessed with it, as if we were the only person in the world who had such a problem. This is clearly not the case. Millions of people have the same problem. This way of thinking makes the problem seem worse than it really is. We're making a mountain out of molehill, and we're also making ourselves feel alone and isolated.

To counteract this tendency, it's useful to recall that there are many other people who have the same problem or something similar. You can think of people you actually know, or imagine people around the world who have this problem. It's also helpful to realize that there are people whose problems are even greater than yours. For example, if you are feeling grief over the loss of a loved one or a relationship that fell apart, you can think of people who have lost several loved ones at once, in a war or natural disaster. This reflection makes the problem seem more like a molehill than a mountain, and thus it becomes more manageable. Even more importantly, it increases your compassion for others.

Cultivating the Four Immeasurables

One of the most powerful, and beautiful, methods found in the Buddha's teachings for transforming our mind is the practice of the four immeasurable thoughts: love, compassion, sympathetic joy, and equanimity. These four attitudes are essential ingredients for our own happiness, peace of mind, and health, as well as for beneficial, satisfying relationships and

interactions with others. Cultivating these thoughts diminishes our habitual attitudes of self-grasping and self-centeredness, which disturb our
peace of mind and lead to problems such as hatred for enemies, envy for
rivals, and clinging to family and friends. These disturbing mental attitudes, if untreated, can lead to physical ailments as well. The four immeasurable thoughts help us overcome these problems and pave the way for
good relations with friend and foe alike.

They are called "immeasurable" for several reasons. One is that we
cultivate these attitudes for all beings, who are so numerous that they cannot be measured or counted. Another is that we create immeasurable positive energy and purify immeasurable negative energy when we cultivate
them. They are also called the four "sublime states" or "divine abodes"
because they represent the ideal way, the most rarefied way, for us to con-
duct ourselves.

The four immeasurable thoughts are expressed in the following
prayer:

> May all beings have happiness and the causes of happiness;
> May all beings be free from suffering and the causes of
>   suffering;
> May all beings never be separated from the happiness that
>   is free from suffering;
> May all beings abide in equanimity, free from attachment
>   and anger that hold some close and others distant.

This verse can be easily memorized and recited from time to time during the day to remind yourself to have positive thoughts for the people
you meet. It will help you develop a heart of kindness toward all beings.
In the next six chapters we explore each of the four immeasurables and
how it can be cultivated. Once you are familiar with the meaning of each
of these and have some familiarity in practicing meditations that cultivate
them, the short verse that summarizes the four will have even deeper
meaning for you.

Practicing the Meditations on the Four Immeasurables

Each of the descriptions of the four immeasurables in this book is followed by one or more meditations—methods for gaining a deeper and more sustained experience of the topics explained. As mentioned above, the main purpose of Buddhist meditation is transforming the mind from negative to positive, and this transformation takes place by making the mind more familiar with positive states, and less familiar with negative ones. By practicing meditation regularly over a period of time, we will have fewer negative thoughts arising in our mind, and more positive ones.

There are many different kinds of meditation, but they can be divided into two main types: placement and analytical.

Placement, or concentration meditation, involves focusing on just one object, such as the breath or a visualized image of the Buddha, without thinking about the object or anything else, and gradually learning to keep the mind concentrated for longer periods of time.

Analytical meditation, on the other hand, involves thinking and analyzing. It is used to recognize mistaken concepts and attitudes that we have—those that cause suffering to ourselves and others—and to familiarize ourselves with correct and beneficial ones. The ultimate purpose of this kind of meditation is to develop the wisdom that sees the true nature of all things.

The meditations in this book are analytical, but while doing them we can also incorporate concentration. If your thinking or analysis gives rise to an experience about the topic you are meditating on—for example, you generate a genuine feeling of loving-kindness—you can stop thinking and just keep your mind focused on that experience for as long as possible. If the feeling fades or your mind wanders, you can then return to the analysis.

When practicing meditation, it is best to sit in a place that is as quiet and free of distractions as possible. Sitting cross-legged is generally most conducive for meditation, but it's not essential. It's perfectly okay to meditate sitting in a chair. Whichever way you sit, however, it's important to keep your back straight, to enable your mind to be more clear and focused.

Begin the meditation with a few minutes of stilling your mind, letting go of all other thoughts and concerns. Focusing on your breath and counting it can help you to do this. Once your mind is calm, generate a positive motivation for doing the meditation—for example, "I want to practice meditation to decrease the negative energy in my mind and to increase my positive qualities such as love, compassion, patience, and wisdom. In this way, I will have more beneficial, positive energy to bring into my interactions with others, and to send out into the world."

Then begin the actual meditation. There is no fixed rule about the length of a meditation session. Initially, you could try meditating for ten or fifteen minutes, but more or less is also fine. You can experiment with varying lengths of time to see what works best for you, according to your ability and schedule. The renowned teacher Lama Yeshe, who founded Kopan Monastery in Nepal, used to say that even five minutes of meditation can be very beneficial. And quality is more important than quantity. A short session in which your mind is very focused is more worthwhile than a long session where your mind is wandering all over the place.

When it is time to end your meditation session, bring what you have thought about and experienced to a positive conclusion. For example, you might resolve to practice loving-kindness with the people you work with, and with your neighbors. And finally, remember the motivation you started with, and dedicate the positive energy you created during the meditation to that same purpose.

The highest form of practicing compassion is the way of the bodhisattvas, those who feel that it's not sufficient to free only themselves from suffering and attain *liberation*, nirvana; they wish to help others become free as well. They cultivate *bodhichitta*: the aspiration to become fully enlightened, to become a Buddha, to help all beings. This is an extraordinarily noble, selfless resolve, but one that we are all capable of cultivating. There are several methods for developing bodhichitta, which involve meditating on topics such as universal love and compassion, the faults of selfishness and benefits of cherishing others, and so on. In fact, most of the ideas and meditations in this book derive from the traditional teachings on how to cultivate bodhichitta. As a result of working on these consistently over a period of time, bodhichitta will arise in us, naturally and spontaneously, and at that point we become bodhisattvas. At times during my presentation of the meditations on the immeasurables, I may mention having the aspiration of bodhichitta as an option, but it is not a requirement for you to begin to discover and cultivate the kind heart that lies within all of us.

Practicing Mind Transformation

Awakening the Kind Heart concludes with a chapter on mental methods we can use to counteract the self-centeredness that thwarts our efforts to truly awaken a kind heart in our day-to-day life. It presents the practice of mind training, also known as thought transformation (*lojong* in Tibetan). Of the many texts in the Buddhist tradition that teach methods for cultivating compassion, some of the most direct and powerful come from the *lojong* tradition, which was first transmitted in Tibet by the great Indian master Atisha. It includes the now well-known practice of *tong-len*, or "taking and giving," the powerful meditation technique that involves imagining that one is *taking* on the suffering of others, and *giving* to them one's own happiness and virtue. Taking-and-giving practice and the other aspects of *lojong* give us incredibly effective and direct methods to undercut the self-cherishing that cuts off compassion.

His Holiness the Dalai Lama encourages the practice of *lojong* and explains it in the following way:

> The essential message of the *lojong* teaching is that if we want
> to see a better world, we should begin by improving our own

mind.... We can spend our life trying to "tame" the world, a task that would never end; or we can take the more practical path of "taming" our own minds. The latter is by far the more effective approach, and brings the most immediate, stable, and lasting solution. It contributes to our own inner happiness, and also contributes to establishing an atmosphere of peace and harmony in the world around us.[3]

In section two of this book, we will explore this wonderful practice in a very pithy way, by going over *The Eight Verses of Thought Transformation*, written by a Tibetan meditator and teacher, Geshe Langri Tangpa, about nine hundred years ago. Each of the eight verses presents an aspect of practicing thought transformation, which you can incorporate in your daily life in a very real and practical way.

Making It Real

Our world desperately needs compassion. If there could be more compassion in people's hearts and lives, if more people could wake up to the realization of compassion and think to themselves, "I don't like being hurt and you don't like being hurt, so let's stop hurting each other," there would be far fewer stories in the news about war, terrorism, violent crimes like murder and rape, child abuse, injustice, and starvation. All the terrible things that humans do to one another, as well as to animals and to our planet, arise from a lack of compassion. It is compassion that keeps us from harming others.

My teacher, Lama Zopa Rinpoche, has pointed out that if we develop compassion for all beings, all beings will be safe from being harmed by us. All beings—or at least, everyone we encounter—will have nothing to fear from us, so indirectly our development of compassion gives them peace. Compassion is also the most effective way to bring about peace in ourselves and in the world.

Genuine compassion cannot be theoretical or hypothetical: "What will I do if…?" It has to arise naturally on the spot. The burning question addressed in this book, then, is *how* to develop and practice compassion in each moment. Practicing the four immeasurables together with the methods of thought transformation included in the eight verses will make compassion as real as our beating heart. In these pages, you will find the way to awaken the kind heart that lies within yourself.

2

Immeasurable Love

May all beings have happiness and the causes of happiness.

Tibetan lamas often begin teaching by saying "All beings want happiness, and do not want to suffer." Accepting this simple truth is the basis of both love and compassion. Every living being has the same essential desire: to stay alive, to feel safe, loved, and appreciated, to satisfy its need for food and shelter, and to have pleasant, positive experiences. The desire for happiness unites all beings, human and non-human. Feeling love for others means acknowledging this desire, respecting it, and doing what we can to fulfill it. This kind of love is sometimes called "loving-kindness" to distinguish it from love that is mixed with lust or selfish attachment. Loving-kindness is pure, unselfish, and unconditional. It is best illustrated by the love of a mother for her child. Out of love she accepts the discomforts of pregnancy, endures the pain of childbirth, and devotes herself twenty-four hours a day to the care of her newborn, expecting nothing in return.

But all of us, even if we are not mothers, have loving-kindness; it is a natural quality of everyone's mind. We feel it most easily and naturally for relatives, friends, small children, or pets. But we can cultivate it further and gradually extend it to more and more people and beings, including strangers and even those who harm us. The ideal in Buddhism is to develop love for *all* living beings without exception.

Immeasurable love means wishing all beings to have happiness and its causes. Such love may sound like a fantasy, but it *has* been attained by others, and we can do it too. We do not have immeasurable love now because of the presence in our mind of ignorance and the other delusions. These obscure our vision, causing us to have negative rather than positive emotions toward others. As we know, however, delusions are not permanent fixtures in our mind. They are transitory and can be eliminated, and once this is done, our mind will be able to feel love for everyone. One of my teachers, Amchog Rinpoche, once said that if we could see the true nature of living beings, we would feel nothing but love and compassion for them.

You might worry that you have only enough love for your family and friends but not for every single living being. "If I try to love everyone, I'll be exhausted!" But you need not worry about that. Love is an inexhaustible energy. Learning to be more loving is like discovering a natural spring within yourself: however much love you give, more will always come bubbling up. It is habitual self-centeredness and self-limiting ways of thinking that constrict the flow of love. As you gradually lessen these, your ability to love will increase.

You will not achieve this immediately, of course. It's a long-term goal, but an attainable one. It is simply a question of making your mind familiar with loving-kindness, and de-familiarizing it with opposing attitudes. Gradually love will arise in your mind more easily and more often.

The Benefits of Cultivating Loving-Kindness

It takes time and effort to develop immeasurable loving-kindness. At times we have enthusiasm for it, but at other times we feel indifferent or just lazy: "Why bother?" Sometimes we may wonder why we should cultivate love for people we don't know, or who have negative attitudes and harm others. Some might even question the whole idea of *cultivating* love, thinking that it should arise all by itself.

These obstacles are easily cut through if we simply contemplate the benefits of practicing loving-kindness. When we see the benefits of growing flowers and vegetables in our garden, we are enthusiastic to do so.

Similarly, by seeing the benefits of cultivating loving-kindness, we want to put our energy into it.

The main purpose of cultivating loving-kindness is not so that *we* will benefit. It is for others, but considering benefits that we will experience can help get us started. If in helping others, we receive benefit as well, is there anything wrong with that? Also, are you even capable of being purely altruistic right now? Can you be completely free of all wants and needs at this moment, and totally dedicate yourself to helping others? If you are honest, you will probably admit that you are not. Even if we are 100% committed to being unselfish and altruistic, it takes time and effort to become that way, and in the meantime, we do have our own needs to fulfill. Practicing loving-kindness and other positive attitudes is actually a way to fulfill our needs: we will be more happy, healthy, and enthusiastic, and less likely to get burned-out and depressed. The Dalai Lama calls this being "wisely selfish"; that is, using our selfish tendencies to act wisely, in ways that bring genuine happiness and benefit to ourselves as well to others. Consider these benefits of loving-kindness, which are commonly presented in Buddhist texts.

YOUR MIND WILL BE HAPPY, AND YOU WILL BE MORE PHYSICALLY HEALTHY.

You can see this for yourself. How does it feel to be angry, hateful, jealous? Is this a pleasant experience? Is your body relaxed and comfortable? Is your mind happy? On the other hand, how does it feel to be loving and kind to others? If you have a choice, which state of mind would you rather have, an angry one or an altruistic, caring one?

YOU WILL BE MORE LOVED, HELPED, AND PROTECTED BY OTHERS.

When you feel love, and treat others with care and kindness, they will naturally feel the same toward you and will be there for you when you need help. This may not work in every case, of course—some people are so full of anger that they may know no other way to respond to your warmth. But if you continue to show them kindness, even they may soften and become more friendly.

YOU WILL SLEEP BETTER AT NIGHT, HAVE MORE PLEASANT DREAMS, AND WAKE UP MORE REFRESHED.

By cultivating positive, loving thoughts for others and being kind in our daily life, at the end of the day your mind will naturally be more at ease, free of stress and regrets. This will enable you to fall asleep and wake up easily, and to have pleasant, even auspicious dreams.

YOUR APPEARANCE WILL START TO BE MORE RADIANT, SMILING, AND RELAXED, AND YOU WILL BE ABLE TO COMMUNICATE MORE EASILY WITH OTHERS.

This is easy to see: hatred makes us ugly, and loving-kindness makes us beautiful. But again, the ideal motive for cultivating loving-kindness is not wanting such results for our own sake, but for the sake of others. If we have a pleasant appearance, people will be attracted to us and will trust us, and thus be more attentive to what we say and do. That puts us in a better position to help them.

YOUR MIND WILL BE MORE SERENE AND EASILY CONCENTRATED, AND YOU WILL MORE EFFORTLESSLY ACCOMPLISH YOUR AIMS.

Hatred, jealousy, and other negative emotions make the mind painfully disturbed, like boiling water, while positive mental states such as loving-kindness make the mind cool and calm. When we try to concentrate—while meditating, reading a book, or doing a task—if we are more habituated with anger and less with loving-kindness, we may be distracted and upset by noise, people, or other beings, so our efforts will not be very successful. By contrast, familiarity with loving-kindness enables us to remain peaceful and focused on what we are doing, no matter what is happening around us. Loving-kindness is an essential component in the cultivation of concentration, which is in turn the gateway to higher states of bliss and peace.

YOU WILL DIE UNCONFUSED.

If you ask yourself what state of mind you would like to have at the time of death—confused, frightened, and angry, or peaceful, positive, and loving—I'm sure you would choose the latter. But in order to be in a positive mental state when you die, you need to familiarize yourself with positive thoughts during your life. And the time to start is *now*, because you don't know when death will happen.

According to Buddhism, our state of mind at death is a major factor determining our next rebirth: dying in a positive state leads to a fortunate rebirth, but dying in a negative state leads to an unfortunate rebirth. This is one of the main reasons why it is so important to work on our mind. But even those who do not accept rebirth would probably wish to die peacefully, painlessly, and with dignity. A nurse who worked with many dying people told me that the people who have the greatest difficulty with pain are those whose minds are negative—fearful, angry, not accepting their death—whereas those whose minds are positive have little or no pain. The way we die depends on the way we have lived.

Spend some time contemplating these benefits. You may not feel that all of them are relevant for you, and you may not experience all of them right away. You may think of other benefits that speak more to your heart. The point is to recognize that learning to be more kind will benefit yourself as well as others, so that you will be inspired to engage in developing loving-kindness.

True Happiness and What Causes It

Love is wishing others to be happy, but what is this "happiness" that we wish others to have? Following a talk I once gave on loving-kindness, a woman put up her hand and asked, "My mother is never satisfied with what she has. She always wants more and more. When I practice loving-kindness for my mother, should I wish her to have all the things she wants?" A good question! When we meditate on loving-kindness, should we wish everyone to be millionaires, with huge mansions, servants, luxury cars, and all the material things they want? Is that the way for them to be happy?

This woman's mother is not unique; probably most people in the world believe that happiness comes from outside: from wealth, material possessions, living in a beautiful home, having a great job, being in a loving relationship with the perfect partner. If this were true, then everyone who has these things would be happy, but this is not the case. There are many examples of attractive, wealthy, famous people who suffer from depression, drug and alcohol addiction, and who even take their own lives. Studies show that people in the West are no happier today than they were fifty years ago, despite the fact that they are wealthier, healthier, live longer, work less, have more leisure time, and travel more. So the usual ideas about what we need to be happy do not seem to be realistic.

In fact, there are different kinds of happiness. The experience most people consider to be happiness is more aptly called "sensory pleasure." This is the pleasure we experience through our five senses: seeing attractive objects, hearing beautiful sounds, smelling nice odors, tasting delicious flavors, and feeling pleasant sensations in our body. These experiences are enjoyable but fleeting, like a dream or a rainbow. They may last a few seconds, minutes, or hours, but then they vanish. They are also untrustworthy, because in order to experience them we rely on external conditions, which we have no control over. If we love the sun, for example, we will be unhappy when the weather is cloudy and rainy.

Another kind of happiness comes from positive states of mind such as

love, compassion, faith, contentment, and gratitude, and from doing beneficial actions such as helping others. This happiness, which we could call
"spiritual happiness," is more pure and stable. Check it out for yourself:
what is more rewarding, buying some new toy for yourself, or giving a gift
to someone else?

So when we generate loving-kindness for people, such as the mother
in the story, who have an insatiable desire for material things, we can wish
them to have more spiritual happiness: inner peace and joy, contentment
with what they have, less greed and selfishness, and more genuine concern
for others. Of course, beings *do* need a certain number of material possessions—it's difficult to be happy if you are hungry and homeless. When
contemplating the wish for others to have happiness, we can start by wishing them to have all the "creature comforts" they need, and then wish
them to have the more pure happiness that comes from positive mental
states and actions.

It is also important to accept that not only does everyone want to be
happy, but everyone *deserves* to be happy. It is our right as beings; we *should*
be happy. We sometimes feel that we do not deserve happiness because we
hurt someone, or because a loved one is suffering. We think, "How can I
be happy when my friend is suffering?" This is guilt, an unhealthy and
deluded mental state. We need to recognize it and learn to avoid it. However, there is a positive counterpart to guilt: regret. If we hurt someone,
it is only right to feel regret, to make amends to the person, and to purify
our karma. But it is unwise to continue beating ourselves up and denying ourselves the right to be happy. Also, if a loved one is suffering, what
good does it do to be miserable? Is that going to help them? Staying positive and cheerful is much more helpful to our loved one, and to everyone else.

Another misconception about the wish for happiness is that it is selfish and greedy, something we should give up. This is not correct; there is
nothing wrong with wanting happiness, but where we often go wrong is
in the kind of happiness we want and what we do to get it. Seeking only
the first kind of happiness—sense pleasures and material wealth—may

bring some short-term happiness, but in the long run leads to problems and dissatisfaction. Furthermore, if in our pursuit of happiness we are self-obsessed and unethical, we can do a lot of damage to ourselves and others, and end up with more suffering than happiness. On the other hand, if we are more interested in the second kind of happiness, and use ethical, skillful means to achieve it, there is no harm done, and everyone will benefit.

The prayer at the head of this chapter also mentions wishing others to have the *causes* of happiness. What are these? If we asked most people, they would probably give a list of things like a nice place to live, a wonderful partner, a satisfying job with a good salary, excellent health, and so on. As we have discussed, a person might have all of these and still be discontented.

According to Buddhism, such things as a nice place to live are conditions for happiness, but not its main causes. The main causes of happiness are positive states of mind and positive actions or karma. If we have these, we will experience happiness, regardless of our external conditions. If we lack these, we won't be happy, even in the best circumstances.

It is important to include the causes of happiness in our kind thoughts toward others, because even if we had the ability to give everyone whatever they needed to be comfortable and happy now, we can't guarantee their future happiness. This is because their happiness in the future depends on their actions and attitudes. Each of us is the creator of our own experiences, good and bad. A person may be comfortable, healthy, and wealthy now, but if he does not live ethically and instead does harmful, unwholesome actions, he is creating the cause of suffering rather than happiness in the future. Therefore, in addition to wishing others to be happy, we also wish them to have the causes of happiness: positive attitudes such as compassion, kindness, and wisdom, and positive actions such as practicing giving, ethics, and patience.

What Prevents Loving-Kindness?

Our efforts to develop loving-kindness are hindered by negative emotions, known in Buddhism as delusions. These disturb our mind, making it unpeaceful and unclear, and also distort our perception, so that we see things in unrealistic ways. Every time a delusion arises, it leaves an imprint or seed in the mind that will give rise to another experience of the same delusion. Our mind is full of these seeds, and when conditions are right, the seeds ripen and we find ourselves feeling angry, attached, jealous, and so on. This situation is not permanent—we can definitely eliminate delusions and their seeds so that they never arise again, but that takes time. In the meantime we can use methods, or antidotes, to deal with them when they arise; we can also learn how to prevent them from arising in the first place. In Buddhist practice, we neither deny negative emotions nor act them out. Either of those approaches just makes things worse! Instead, we acknowledge the existence of negative emotions and work on our mind to reduce them and replace them with positive states.

Let's look at several of the negative emotions that can interfere with our cultivation of love, and consider some antidotes to them.

ANGER AND HATRED

I once met a man who told me that he had been involved in various peace groups for thirty years, working for peace in the world. These groups were not very effective because there was so much fighting: the members of one group would fight with each other, and there were conflicts between one group and another. We probably all have similar experiences. We start off with good intentions—in a relationship, at work, or as a volunteer for an aid organization—only to have our dreams shattered by negative emotions such as anger. The lesson is clear: if we want to have more peace, kindness, harmony, and happiness in our relationships, our community, and in the world, we need to start by working on our own minds. Anger is one of the greatest obstacles to peace in the world, and also one of the greatest obstacles to cultivating loving-kindness. In fact, it is the very opposite to love. It is impossible to have both anger and love in our mind at the same time toward the same person.

Anger is defined as a mental factor that perceives its object as unattractive, exaggerates its unattractiveness, becomes antagonistic, and wishes to harm the object. For example, when we are angry at someone, our mind focuses on certain disagreeable qualities or unskillful actions we observe in him, and exaggerates these such that the person appears 100% negative, lacking any positive qualities. We then cling to this image, believing the person to really be like that, permanently, for all of time. In reality, our view of this person is distorted because no one is completely bad, but blinded by anger we can't see his good side. We may then have thoughts of harming the person, physically, verbally, or mentally, and if we act these out, we create enormous problems, for ourselves and others.

Some people think they don't have anger because they don't lose their temper, scream, and act aggressively. If you have this idea, it might be good to observe your mind more carefully. There are milder forms of anger we are all prone to, such as irritation, impatience, frustration, criticalness, and aversion. Also, anger can play a leading role in other dramas like disappointment, hurt, depression, fear, grief, shyness, and guilt. These mental states are not as destructive as full-blown anger, but could become so if we don't deal with them and instead let them grow. And they do cause damage: they make our mind troubled and unhappy, and inhibit us from being as respectful and kind to others as we could.

Some people feel anger is natural, and that we should let ourselves experience it and express it whenever it arises. Fire, too, is natural, but don't we control it to prevent terrible damage? Also, expressing anger may give some immediate relief, but what about the long-term consequences, for ourselves and others? Expressing anger easily becomes a habit. As a result, anger arises more frequently and easily. The problem just gets worse.

The Buddhist teachings contain many antidotes that help us to neither suppress anger nor act it out, but rather to work on it within our mind, learning how to transform our mental state from negative to positive. Here a few for you to consider.

Recognize the harm done by anger.
If we don't see anger as destructive, we are likely to get caught up in it instead of counteracting it. This is especially so when we are already angry, as it tends to be self-justifying: "It's right for me to be angry at her; she did something really wrong." If a fire broke out in our house, we would do everything possible to put it out because we know clearly how destructive it can be. Similarly if we can clearly see the destructiveness of anger, we will put it out as soon as it arises in our mind.

Consider the following problems that arise from anger: it is harmful to our physical and mental health, causes our mind to be disturbed and unclear, and can motivate us to speak or act hurtfully to others, including our loved ones. Lama Zopa Rinpoche says that delusions such as anger torture us. If we carefully check our mental state when we are angry, we can see that this is so. Why do we allow ourselves to be tortured?

There are also subtler, more long-term effects of anger. Getting angry, especially if we act it out, creates unskillful karma that will bring painful experiences in the future. And it destroys much of the good karma we have worked so hard to accumulate. It is a major obstacle to the cultivation of the positive qualities we need to progress along the spiritual path and thus attain higher states such as liberation and enlightenment.

If you recognize the harm done by anger, resolve to not let yourself be hijacked by it when it arises, and instead employ methods to transform your mind into a positive state.

Think about karma, the reality of cause and effect.
If someone hurts or disturbs you, look back and see if you can recall doing something that may have provoked the person to behave this way. If you can't think of anything, consider the possibility that you may have done something to this person in a past life, and thus you have a "karmic debt" to pay. If this idea makes sense to you, accept the responsibility for this

present situation, and resolve to refrain from behaving harmfully from now on. In this way you will avoid creating future problems for yourself and others.

Regard the person you're angry at as a mirror.
The Buddhist teachings say that we would not see faults in others if we did not have faults in ourselves. If we feel critical or angry at someone, it could be that the person is showing us something about ourselves we do not like. To counteract this problem, we must learn to accept the existence of that quality in ourselves, with patience and kindness.

I sometimes feel annoyed by noisy, chatty people. I have the concept that people should be quiet, calm, and subdued. That is how I try to be, but when I look honestly at my mind, I realize that it's very noisy and chatty, almost constantly making comments about everyone and everything. Chattiness, in fact, is a quality of my own mind, but I don't like it and try to keep it hidden. When I see it in others I feel judgmental: "You shouldn't be that way!" By working on being more accepting and tolerant of my inner chattiness, I can learn to be more accepting of that quality in others.

Try this: bring to mind a person you feel angry or annoyed at, and ask yourself what exactly it is that you dislike in him or her. Once you have identified that, check: "Is this something that I have in myself? Have I ever behaved like that?" If you *are* able to find in yourself the same thing (or something similar) that you don't like in the other person, the solution is to learn acceptance and forgiveness toward yourself. When you can be more tolerant and compassionate toward yourself, with whatever faults you have, you will be better able to accept others as they are, and less likely to get angry at them.

Difficult people can teach us patience.
If we are sincere about working on ourselves—decreasing our ego, anger, and other delusions, and increasing patience, love, and other positive qualities—then someone who arouses our anger is like a teacher, giving us a

chance to learn that we still have a lot of work to do. Think of a time when difficulties with another person taught you important lessons. Resolve that when you again encounter problems with people, you will use these as opportunities for growth. It's possible that you may end up feeling grateful for the difficult people in your life!

Keep your mind contented.
Anger is more likely to arise in your mind when you are unhappy or dissatisfied. If you notice yourself getting irritated by even small things, sit down and check what's going on in the deeper levels of your mind. Are there unhappy, critical thoughts about yourself or aspects of your life? Are you focusing more on the negative side of things rather than the positive side? If so, remember that there *are* good things about you and your life; bring some of these to mind, recognize your good fortune, and generate a feeling of contentment, satisfied with what you have and are.

ATTACHMENT

Another obstacle to love is attachment. This may sound strange to some people, because attachment and love are often seen as identical. But attachment is very different from love. It is a delusion, a negative mental state, a cause of suffering; whereas love is a positive mental state, a cause of happiness.

Part of the confusion may be in how we define the word. According to Buddhism "attachment" is defined as a mental factor that perceives its object as attractive, exaggerates its attractiveness, regards it as a cause of happiness, and wants to possess and retain it. So, like anger, it has an unrealistic image of its object, which can be anything—a person, thing, place, idea, activity, and so on. While anger exaggerates the negative side of its object, attachment exaggerates the positive side. For example, when we meet an attractive, interesting person, attachment creates an image of the person as being totally perfect, the one I've been looking for all my life, able to make me happy forever. This is sheer fantasy, because in samsara no one is completely perfect. And even if we found someone who was 99% perfect, she would not be able to make us happy forever because she will inevitably change, get old, and die. Furthermore, as our mind can change too, we might lose interest in her and meet someone else we find more appealing.

Therefore, one fault of attachment is that it doesn't see things as they are; it sees things in exaggerated, unrealistic ways. Because of that it leads to disappointment and suffering, rather than the happiness we wish for. Another fault of attachment is that it is based on self-centeredness. We tend to see everything in terms of "I"—what *I* like and don't like, what makes *me* feel good and bad, who treats *me* the way I want, and who does not, and so forth. With this egotistical approach, we want to be close to people who make us feel good, treat us the way we want, and do what we think they should do. This is the main difference between attachment and love. Attachment is concerned about *me*: my happiness, my needs and wishes. Love, on the other hand, is concerned about the other person's needs, wishes, and happiness. Attachment sees others in terms of how they help me and make me feel good; love sees others as they are, deserving of love just because they exist. We probably have a mixture of both love and attachment in our relationships with others. What we need to do is reduce our attachment and increase our love. Our relationships will become healthier and less problematic as a result.

It takes a long time and a lot of work to become free from selfishness and attachment. In the meantime, there are some remedies we can use to decrease attachment and create more space in our mind for pure, unselfish love.

Contemplate the faults of attachment.
If we see nothing wrong with attachment, we won't even try to work on it, so an important first step is to recognize the problems it brings. For one thing, being a delusion, it disturbs our mind. Check your own experience: when you have attachment to someone or something, how does it affect your mind? You probably feel excitement, which can be mistaken for

happiness, but check more carefully. Is it real, stable happiness, or are you excited about imaginary experiences you hope to have in the future with your object of attachment? These experiences might not happen, so how will you feel about that? Recall past experiences of attachment, and check how they ended up. Did they lead to lasting happiness and satisfaction, or to disappointment and pain?

Attachment can also lead to other painful and disturbing emotions: *fear* of not getting or losing our object of attachment; *disappointment, grief,* and *pain* when what we fear does happen; *anger* if the object doesn't live up to our expectations; *jealousy* toward a person who has some desired object that we don't have; *pride* that we have more than others, and so on.

Remember impermanence.

This is the most effective remedy to attachment. Everything—people, beings, objects, the world itself—is changing every moment and will one day go out of existence. The object of your attachment will not always be as attractive as it is now. Imagine how it will look ten years from now… twenty years from now … fifty years from now … and check if your feelings about it remain the same. How would you feel if you lost it altogether? The pleasure you experience is impermanent, too. How long does the pleasure you experience with an object last?

Don't be surprised if you encounter internal resistance to thinking about these ideas. This happens because our mind is usually controlled by attachment, which wants things to be permanent: always there, never changing. Reflecting on the impermanent nature of things is an insult to attachment; it doesn't like it at all! If you can recognize that attachment is a delusion that creates suffering rather than happiness, you will find the courage to ignore its objections, and develop a more realistic way of looking at things. It might be best to start contemplating the impermanence of objects you are not so attached to, such as material things, and gradually work on more difficult objects, such as people.

As our attachment to people and things lessens, this doesn't mean we won't like them anymore and will want to get rid of them. On the contrary, we can continue to enjoy them, but without attachment; this actually means we will cherish them even more.

See objects of desire more realistically.
Since attachment exaggerates the good qualities of an object, it's helpful to think of its negative aspects, to have a more balanced perspective. For example, if you think, "If I had a BMW, I would be so happy!" contemplate the problems of owning such a car—the expenses, the maintenance, and the worry that it could be stolen or damaged. Or, if you feel attracted toward someone and think that having a relationship with him would bring perfect happiness, remember that the person may have faults you don't see right now, or that you might run into conflicts later on. But be careful to not go too far and develop aversion for the person. Just try to see him in a more realistic way, as someone who has both good and bad qualities.

SELFISHNESS

Another factor that interferes with the development of pure love is self-centeredness: our habitual preoccupation with our own self, feeling that our own needs and wishes are of primary importance, and those of others are of little or no importance. For example, it is selfishness that thinks: "My happiness is more important than anyone else's. Never mind if one billion people don't have enough to eat. I want the best food and I want it prepared in the right way, and if it's not, I have the right to be unhappy and complain." We would never actually say this, or even think such thoughts on the conscious level, but if we look deeper into our mind, we do have such feelings—particularly when we're not happy with the food sitting on the plate in front of us. Thinking of ourselves all the time makes it hard to cultivate genuine concern for others.

Self-centeredness can also contaminate the work we do to benefit others. A few days into a retreat I was leading, one of the participants came to me in tears. She told me that she had been doing volunteer work to help children, and thought that her motivation was an altruistic one, but now, seeing her mind more clearly during the retreat, she realized that her motive was to receive love from them. It's understandable that we feel dismayed, like this woman, when we discover ulterior motives behind actions we supposedly do for the benefit of others. But there's no point being upset—that doesn't help. Instead we can use this experience to learn and grow.

For one thing, we can be thankful that we recognize our selfishness. Probably most people in the world are driven by self-centeredness without even realizing it, and even those who do realize it may think there's nothing wrong with it. So it's actually admirable to acknowledge and regret being selfish. Secondly, if we ask ourselves if our motivation is pure 100% selfishness, we will probably find that it's mixed: although there is some selfishness, there is also some concern for others. If we had zero concern for others, we probably wouldn't even think about doing things to help them. It's important to recognize this; otherwise we may feel hopeless—"I'm completely selfish; everything I do is only for myself, and I will always be this way." If we think like that, we are denying the innate love, compassion, and positive qualities that do exist in our hearts. We need to get to know our mind, learn to distinguish the negative from the positive, and feel confident that we can decrease the negative qualities and increase the positive. The situation is not hopeless. It just takes time.

Why are we selfish? According to Buddhism, selfishness derives from the ignorance that believes in a real, permanent, independently existing I or ego. We grasp at our *I* as being the most important thing in the world, and all our thoughts, feelings, and actions revolve around it—trying to keep it happy, and to keep away any problems. This attitude leads to other disturbing emotions: *anger*, when we don't get what we want, or are not treated respectfully; *attachment*, wanting to possess and control the people and things that make us feel good and support our ego; *fear*, when our sense of self-importance is threatened; *arrogance*, feeling we are better than others and have the right to mistreat them.

Being centered on ego interferes with the development of pure, unconditional love and compassion because it causes us to discriminate others according to whether they help us, harm us, or do nothing for us. It is the greatest hindrance to enlightenment. It says in the teachings that there was a time, many lifetimes ago, when the Buddha and ourselves were equal: both were beings suffering in samsara. But the Buddha became enlightened long ago, and we are still beings suffering in samsara. Why? Because the Buddha decided to give up his self-centered attitude, but we did not. Consider using the remedies to selfishness below to decrease your reliance on ego as your central reference point. (Section two of this book presents a variety of methods for overcoming selfishness that can be combined with and complement the contemplations below.)

Contemplate the faults of selfishness.
We will have more enthusiasm to work on reducing our self-concern if we can clearly see what's wrong with it. Contemplate these points, thinking of examples from your own experience: Selfishness motivates us to do negative actions such as stealing or saying hurtful words, and thus we create negative karma, which will bring problems in the future. All the problems we experience in this life are the result of negative karma we created in our past lives, motivated by selfishness. Selfishness causes problems in our relationships, at work, and even when we're by ourselves: it underlies our feelings of loneliness, boredom, anxiety, and depression. Selfishness makes us reluctant to meditate or do other spiritual activities, and thus we miss opportunities to create the causes for more pure, sublime happiness.

Ask yourself who is more important: me or others?
This is a method recommended by the Dalai Lama. We all accept that in a democratic society, the wishes of the majority take precedence over those of the minority. But when it comes to ourselves and others we are not very democratic, because even though I am only one person and oth-

ers are countless, we regard our wishes and needs as more important than those of others. Is this right?

Try this simple meditation: imagine yourself sitting in front of you, on one side. Think about the problems you have, your needs and wishes. Then, on the other side imagine a number of other people and contemplate the problems they experience. Then, ask yourself: is it right for me to be more concerned about that one person, me, than about all those other people? Am I really more important than those other people? If your mind replies: "But it's normal to be mainly more concerned with self than with others; that's what everyone does," check if that is true. Don't parents take care of their children? Don't teachers take care of their students? Don't doctors and nurses take care of people who are sick? Imagine what the world would be like if no one ever did anything for anyone else. Finally, contemplate that others' wish to be happy and free from suffering is exactly the same as yours.

Cultivate a motivation that puts others first.
There is always a motivation behind the things we do, and most of the time it's related to selfishness. Everything we do is an attempt to fulfill our own wish to be happy and avoid problems. There is nothing wrong with this wish, but trying to fulfill it in a self-centered way will bring only frustration and disappointment. One way we can change this situation is to change our motivation, and cultivate the intention that we are doing things for others, not only for ourselves. You can think, "I am doing this in order to attain enlightenment so that I can help all beings become free of suffering and attain enlightenment as well." However, if you are not comfortable with the idea of attaining enlightenment, another possibility is thinking that you want to help others in this present life as much as possible. You can think, "I wish to make my life beneficial for others, and that is why I am doing this action." Feel free to play around with this idea and find a way of cultivating an altruistic motivation that feels right for you. You can do it at the start of any activity—working, meditating, eating, playing, sleeping, going to the doctor, and so on. If it is difficult

to remember to do it before every action, at least spend a few minutes cultivating such a motivation at the start of your day.

Don't Forget to Be Kind to Yourself

As you embark on the meditations to cultivate loving-kindness in the following chapter, don't forget to have loving-kindness for yourself. You are also a living being who deserves and needs love and compassion. In fact, you can't really love others until you learn to love yourself. That doesn't mean being selfish and egotistical. It means being a friend to yourself, accepting yourself as you are with your faults and limitations, knowing that you can change and grow.

It's no use hating yourself because you are not the way you would like to be, or beating your head against the wall every time you make a mistake. Doing this only adds more problems to those you already have, and does not help you to improve. But having a kind heart toward yourself lightens the pain of failures and faults, provides the space in which you can grow, and lays a good basis for loving relationships with others.

3
Meditations on Loving-Kindness

I have learned that even the most vicious, degenerate person is capable of boundless compassion, kindness, and generosity. I have witnessed individuals do the totally unexpected, for the benefit of others, even at the risk of their own life.
—An inmate who has spent over thirty years
in a maximum-security prison

The meditations in this chapter will help you to develop love. Many, many practitioners over many centuries have discovered the kind heart that lies within them by using meditations such as these, which make use of factors known to help loving-kindness arise in our hearts. The first meditation—A Basic Meditation on Loving-Kindness—utilizes the awareness that every being wants happiness, just as we do, and that all beings deserve to be happy. In that meditation, we bring to mind specific people or beings, contemplate their desire for happiness, and generate the wish for them to be happy.

Another factor that induces loving-kindness is *gratitude*. When someone helps us or treats us kindly, particularly at a time when we desperately need help, it is natural to feel grateful to this person, deeply thankful for her kindness. We also wish to repay that person's kindness—if she were ever in need of anything, we would be more than happy to offer our help. These feelings are the basis for the second meditation, on the kindness of others.

A third factor that can arouse loving-kindness is *seeing loving-kindness in someone else.* Just as others serve as mirrors reflecting our negative qualities, they also mirror our positive qualities. When we see someone who is kind and compassionate toward others, we feel touched and inspired to be like that ourselves. This is a sign that loving-kindness already exists within us; otherwise, we would not recognize it in others. This phenomenon is the basis for the third meditation, which involves visualizing Maitreya—the Buddha who embodies perfect, universal loving-kindness for all beings, the very quality we are trying to cultivate. Visualizing the Buddha and contemplating the pure, unconditional love that he feels for all beings without exception can help us to get in touch with such feelings in our own hearts. He also serves as a role model, showing us what we can become. The meditation is explained in terms of Maitreya Buddha, but if you prefer, you can visualize another figure or image that signifies for your mind the quality of universal love.

At the end of each meditation, you are asked to "dedicate the merit." This is a traditional practice that is done at the end of any practice session (or any other activity that generates benefit). It involves considering any goodness or "merit" we have developed or accrued and giving it away, so that we don't fall into the habit of hoarding the goodness that arises from our practice. It is always dedicated to the benefit of everyone.

People sometimes report that they do not feel anything when they try to meditate on loving-kindness. They repeat the words to themselves, but their mind feels blank, empty. This is actually normal, especially when we are new to the practice. Part of the problem is that we have expectations: in the back of our mind we are hoping for some fantastic experience. For example, we hope that our mind will be suffused with blissful love for all beings everywhere. And if that doesn't happen we feel let down, disappointed, and may even think that the practice doesn't work.

Lama Yeshe used to say to us, "Don't have any expectations when you meditate." It's quite hard to do this, because our normal tendency is to expect results from the things that we put effort into. So, when we take up meditation, we do so hoping for wonderful, blissful, feelings flowing through our body and mind. The irony is that having expectations in meditation is counterproductive, an obstacle to attaining its results. If we grasp at wonderful experiences, we are pushing them further away. It's when we can relax and just do the practice without expecting anything that the results will come.

Try not to have expectations, as Lama Yeshe advised. Just do the practices, repeat the words of the meditation to yourself, and accept whatever happens in your mind. Of course, it is okay to *try* to generate the feeling of loving-kindness, but don't worry if nothing seems to happen. Expecting instant results from meditation is like expecting that flowers and vegetables will appear in your garden right after you plant the seeds. Things don't happen like that. You need to look after your garden, nurture the tiny shoots when they appear, and wait patiently. Eventually, when the time is right, the results will come.

Just so, after planting the seeds of loving thoughts in your mind for a while, you will begin to notice small, subtle positive thoughts and feelings arising spontaneously, of their own accord. If you nurture them and continue doing the practice, they will arise more frequently, both during and outside of formal meditation practice.

A Basic Meditation on Loving-Kindness

The meditation is divided into five parts: loving-kindness for a friend, a neutral person, an enemy, yourself, and all beings. The number of parts you meditate on in each session can vary, according to the amount of time you have, your ability to sustain your mind in a meditative state, as well as your needs at any given time. For example, if you are having difficulty with someone at work and wish to generate loving-kindness for him or her, you might want to focus on just that person.

Also, you can sometimes alter the sequence of the parts. Some teachers recommend that you start meditating on loving-kindness for yourself, then a friend, and so on; others recommend putting yourself last. There are no hard and fast rules. Feel free to experiment with different sequences to find what works best for you.

PREPARATION

Sit comfortably. Relax your body and mind and let all thoughts and worries subside. Mindfully observe your breath until you are calm and your awareness is focused in the here and now.

MOTIVATION

Think that you are doing this meditation for the benefit of yourself and others, to generate more positive, loving energy in your mind and to send it out to others, to the world. If you are comfortable with the idea of bodhichitta discussed in chapter 1, you can think you are doing it in order to become enlightened so that you can help all beings in the best way.

MAIN MEDITATION

It is helpful to begin by generating a feeling of love in your heart. You can do this by thinking of someone you find easy to love—a relative or friend, a small child or a pet—and letting your natural good feelings for this person (or being, in the case of an animal) arise in your heart. You might like to imagine your love as a warm, bright light or energy glowing in your heart. Then bring to mind one or more of the following persons and do your best to extend this feeling of loving-kindness to them.

Loving-kindness for a friend
A "friend" is someone we find easy to like and feel close to—it can be an acquaintance, a partner, or a family member. However, it best initially to not think of someone for whom you have romantic love or sexual desire; otherwise, those feelings may arise and hinder your ability to distinguish love from attachment. You can visualize the person sitting in front of you, or in the place he or she is right now. Contemplate that this person has, deep in his or her heart, the wish to be happy. Feel that the person

deserves to be happy. Generate the wish that this person could have the happiness he or she longs for.

If you like, you can think or say to yourself phrases such as: "May you be happy. May you be safe, free from harm and danger. May you have all that you need to be truly happy, peaceful, and satisfied. May all your thoughts and actions be positive, and all your experiences good." You can modify these phrases, using whatever words enable you to generate genuine loving-kindness.

If you imagined your loving-kindness as light or energy, you can visualize it radiating from your heart to this person. Let them become filled with it. It is also effective to imagine the person receiving what they need to be happy, such as the food they like to eat, a comfortable place to live, pleasant encounters with other people, positive thoughts and feelings in their mind, and so on.

Spend as much time as you wish meditating on loving-kindness for this person, and then you can bring to mind another friend and do the same reflection with that person. Alternatively, you can do one of the other parts of the practice below, or conclude your meditation with the dedication.

Loving-kindness for a neutral person

A neutral person is someone we neither like nor dislike. It could be a neighbor or someone we work with whom we are not close to. Imagine such a person in front of you, and contemplate that this person, like yourself and your friends, simply wants to be happy. Feel that this person deserves to be happy. Generate the wish that he or she could be happy.

Then you can repeat the phrases, or whatever words you find most effective: "May you be happy. May you be safe, free from harm and danger. May you have all that you need to be truly happy, peaceful, and satisfied. May all your thoughts and actions be positive, and all your experiences good."

Imagine the light or energy of your loving-kindness radiating from your heart to this person, filling him or her. And imagine the person receiving what he or she needs to be happy.

Loving-kindness for an enemy

"Enemy" is quite a heavy word, and we may think we have no enemies because there's no one we really hate and wish to harm. But it can simply mean someone we close our heart to; someone we dislike or find irritating. Bring to mind such a person; it could be someone you know, or a public figure like a politician. If you are relatively new to this part of the practice, and if there *is* someone you strongly hate, it's better not to use that person. Start with someone toward whom your feelings are more low-level, and you can gradually work your way up to the more challenging people. Imagine the person in front of you, and contemplate that he or she, like yourself and your friends, simply wants to be happy. Feel that the person deserves to be happy. Generate the wish that the person could be happy. (In case anger arises in your mind instead of love, you can use one or more of the methods for dealing with anger explained in the previous chapter. If and when your negative feelings subside, you can continue with the loving-kindness meditation.)

Then you can repeat the following phrases, or whatever words you find most effective: "May you be happy. May you be safe, free from harm and danger. May you have all that you need to be truly happy, peaceful, and satisfied. May all your thoughts and actions be positive, and all your experiences good."

Imagine the light or energy of your loving-kindness radiating from your heart to this person, filling him or her. Imagine that the person receives what he or she needs to be happy.

Loving-kindness for oneself

To be able to truly love others, you need to love yourself. Loving yourself means accepting yourself as you are, with your present faults and shortcomings. It means being kind to yourself, being a friend to yourself, rather than being angry and frustrated that you aren't the person you'd like to be. It also means acknowledging your potential to change and grow, to experience greater happiness, peace, and positive qualities. And it involves giving yourself the space to fulfill that potential, and truly wishing yourself to be happy and free from problems.

Contemplate that you are a being who wishes to be happy and that you deserve to be happy. Then, really wish yourself all the happiness and goodness there is. "May I be happy. May I be safe, free from harm and danger. May I have all that I need to be truly happy, peaceful, and satisfied. May all my thoughts and actions be positive, and all my experiences good." Imagine that the warm energy of loving-kindness in your heart radiates out, gradually filling your body and mind, and you become suffused with happiness and its causes.

Loving-kindness for all beings
Send loving-kindness to all other living beings—human beings and non-human beings such as animals. You may like to think especially of those who are going through extreme difficulties such as war, sickness, poverty, hunger, fear, oppression, and so forth. Think, and feel sincerely: "May all beings everywhere be happy. May they be safe, free from harm and danger. May they have all they need to be truly happy, peaceful, and satisfied. May all their thoughts and actions be positive, and all their experiences good."

Feel the gentle energy of loving-kindness radiate out from your heart to all living beings, everywhere in the universe. Imagine that it gives them comfort, relieves them of their mental and physical suffering, and helps them to experience happiness and peace of mind.

DEDICATION

When you are ready to conclude the meditation, dedicate the positive energy of your meditation to all beings, intently wishing that they find happiness and, ultimately, enlightenment.

A Meditation on the Kindness of Others

This meditation has several parts; do as many parts as you have time and energy for in each session. You can also reflect on these ideas in your daily life, when you observe people working on a road, for example, or constructing a building, or making deliveries. Think about the benefit these people provide to you and others, recognize their kindness, and wish them to be well and happy.

Note: The first part of this meditation involves reflecting on the kindness of your mother. As we discussed above, mothers are one of the best examples of unconditional love, the kind of love we are trying to cultivate in our own hearts. However, some mothers are neglectful, and others are even abusive. If that is the case with your mother, and thinking of her brings up only hurt and anger, then you can replace her with a different person, someone who did give you love and care: your father, a grandparent, aunt or uncle, or a teacher.

PREPARATION

Make yourself comfortable in a good position for meditation. Try to keep your back straight, but let the other parts of your body be relaxed. Let your mind settle down in the present; let go of all thoughts and decide to keep your mind focused on the meditation.

MOTIVATION

Generate an altruistic motivation for doing the meditation; for example, aspiring to attain enlightenment for the benefit of all beings, or wanting to make your life as meaningful and beneficial to others as possible.

MAIN MEDITATION

The kindness of your mother

Become aware of your body. At this point in your life, your body is fully developed (or nearly so), strong, and able to take care of itself. But your body was not always like this. At the beginning of your life, it was small, helpless, and completely dependent on others for survival. The person who helped you the most at that time was your mother. Your mother is also responsible for the very existence of your body. Most of us cannot remember our birth or the first months and years of our life, but we can use our imagination to picture ourselves as a small baby and the experiences we had at that time.

Your body actually began as a tiny fertilized egg in your mother's womb. Imagine your mother at the time she was pregnant with you, carrying you in her womb. It was probably not an easy time. She may have experienced discomfort, nausea, and even pain. She had to make adjustments in her lifestyle—giving up activities or foods that she liked, and doing other things that she did not like. She may have felt embarrassment about her appearance, the changes in her figure, and the clothing she had to wear. But she put up with these difficulties for your sake, out of love for you. Contemplate what your mother did for you during this time, and feel grateful for her kindness.

During the time of your actual birth, she probably experienced terrible pain, not just for a few minutes but for many hours. In addition to the pain there may also have been fear, because during childbirth the child, the mother, or both can die or be severely hurt. Contemplate how she went through these difficulties for you.

After birth, your mother had the job of taking care of you—a fulltime job! Imagine yourself as a newborn baby, tiny, helpless, unable to do anything for yourself. Every few hours, when you cried out of hunger, she fed you with milk from her breasts, bathed you, changed your diapers, and dressed you in clean clothes. When you were not sleeping, you probably did not like being alone, so she spent time holding you, giving you attention and affection, talking to you, and playing with you.

Your mother was also your first teacher. Now you are independent and able to do everything on your own, but in the early part of your life, the only things you could do were to lie on your back, wave your arms and legs in the air, cry, drink milk, and make a smelly mess in your diapers. Slowly, gradually, you had to learn how to feed yourself, drink from a cup, crawl, walk, talk, dress yourself, use a toilet, bathe yourself, and so on. These are simple tasks, but we were not able to learn them on our own; we needed a lot of patient help from our mother and others who cared for us.

Think of other examples of kindness and help you received from your mother over the years, as you grew older and started going to school. She may have taken you to school, picked you up afterward, helped you with your homework, took you to friends' houses and to music lessons, prepared your meals, washed your clothes, and so on ad infinitum. It's also useful to realize that she did all this work without pay, simply out of love. People usually expect wages for the work they do, but although a mother's job is 24 hours a day, 7 days a week, 365 days a year, she received no salary.

Even when you became older and more independent, she was always there to help: when you had emotional crises, relationship problems, or financial difficulties. At times you may have felt that she was the only person in the world you could turn to and trust.

If you have memories of your mother's unkindness—if she was sometimes unfair, got angry at you, or punished you—or if you feel that she didn't do her job well, contemplate that she is just an ordinary human being, not a buddha! Being a mother is difficult and demanding, and it's only natural that mothers sometimes experience anger, frustration, and depression. (One woman told me that becoming a mother enabled her to heal her relationship with her own mother, because she realized firsthand how hard the job is, and how much her mother did for *her* when she was small.) You can also reflect that your mother was not always an adult: she was once a child, too, and went through difficulties with her parents, at school, and so on. Seeing her as a human being who has her own difficulties and problems will help you to forgive her.

By contemplating these points, if a feeling of gratitude and the wish to repay your mother's kindness arises in your heart, you can stop thinking and let your mind stay focused on that feeling as long as you can.

The kindness of your father and other relatives

You can then contemplate other people who were important in the early part of your life, and what they did for you. Your father may well have been the "breadwinner," working hard to provide the necessities for his family. He may not have enjoyed his job—it may have been stressful, exhausting, or unrewarding—and sometimes he may have come home in a bad mood. In spite of the difficulties of his life, he probably spent time playing with you, helping you with your homework, or taking you to movies or sports events. Think about what your father did for you, and generate gratitude for his kindness. Do the same with other family members who helped to care for you, teach you, play with you, and so on.

The kindness of teachers

At this point in our life we know many things and have many skills, but we were not born with these. We learned them from others. Most of our knowledge came from our teachers in school. As children, we may have complained about some of our teachers, thinking that they did not do their job well. We probably even made fun of them. But we need to recognize that the work they do is essential, and not easy. Imagine trying to discipline and teach a roomful of restless children, many of whom are not even interested in learning. And imagine how your life would be if you had not received an education. This is actually the case for many children in the world. Contemplate how fortunate you are that you *did* have a chance to learn from your teachers. Thanks to them, you now have the knowledge and skills you need to function in the world, get a job and support yourself, travel, and so forth. Feel grateful for their kindness, and wish them to be happy.

The kindness of those who provide us with food,
clothing, lodging, and so on

Everything we have, use, and enjoy, including the very things we need to stay alive, are provided by others. Think about the last meal you ate, and all the people who made that meal possible: the farmers who grew the grains and vegetables, others who helped to harvest it, truck drivers who transported it, and people who worked in the factories and markets to process, package, and sell the food. So many people and so many months are required to produce just one plate of food. If your diet includes meat, eggs, and dairy products, then animals were also involved; most of them probably experienced suffering in the farms where they lived, and some were even killed. We never meet most of the beings who provide our food, but we benefit greatly from their work. In fact, we could not survive without it. Contemplate this, feel grateful to them, and generate the wish for them to be happy.

The same is true for everything else in our life: the clothes and shoes we wear; the house or apartment we live in; the buildings in which we work, study, shop, and play; the books we read; the cars we drive; the music and films we enjoy; and also public services, water, electricity, gas, and so on. Contemplate how we are dependent on others for all these things. Appreciate the kindness of all those people, and wish them to be happy.

If your mind objects, "Wait a minute. I pay for all these things, so *I* am helping *them*, doing a service for *them*," this may be true, but where does your money come from? Did you have it when you were born? Either you inherited it, or it was given to you by your employer or customers for the work you do; in both cases, it came from others. And even if you earned it yourself, you depend on others for that to happen: the teachers from whom you acquired the knowledge and skills needed to get a job, your parents who paid for your education, the employer who hires you, the clients who enable the company to keep running, and so on. Is there anything that you can claim to be inherently, rightfully yours, without depending on others?

Or you may think, "Farmers, shopkeepers, and so on are not working out of kindness for me, they are working to take care of themselves and their families." To counteract this thought, you can ask yourself: can I know for sure what is going on in other peoples' minds, what their motivation is? If you cannot, then it's not fair to judge them. It's possible that the people who produce the things you use *do* have an altruistic attitude. Moreover, it doesn't really matter what their motivation is; our ability to receive benefit from others does not depend on their motivation. For example, the sun does not have the motivation to benefit us, but we receive enormous benefit from it: light, warmth, power, energy for plants to grow, and so on. Recognize and appreciate what others do for you, and wish them to have happiness and only good experiences.

The kindness of those who help us on the spiritual path
In order to attain higher states such as enlightenment, and also to ensure that we have fortunate lives and experiences on the way to enlightenment, we need to create the right causes: positive states of mind and good karma. And to create these causes, we depend on others. For example, *giving* is one of the best ways to create good karma. There are different ways to practice giving: giving resources such as money and food, giving protection from fear and danger, giving love, and giving spiritual advice and teachings. To practice any of these, we need recipients, other beings who receive our gifts. We cannot practice giving without other beings, thus they are kind to provide us with opportunities to cultivate this beautiful, heart-expanding practice.

Another way that others help us on the spiritual path is by enabling us to practice *ethics*, or benevolent behavior. In Buddhism, ethics involves refraining from harmful actions with our body, speech, and mind. In order to engage fully in this practice, we need the presence of other beings we could harm, but we consciously refrain from doing so. Therefore, beings are kind to serve as objects for our practice of ethics.

The practice of *patience* involves learning to manage anger and keep our mind calm and balanced with difficult people and situations. We all have patience to a certain extent, but we need to increase it so that we can remain undisturbed by more and more challenging people. To learn how to do this, we need people who make us angry, so that we can see how much anger we still have, and how much work we have yet to do to be truly patient. Thus even annoying or hurtful beings are kind to us, giving us opportunities to practice patience.

Other beings are also essential factors in our cultivation of loving-kindness, compassion, equanimity, and bodhichitta. It would be very difficult to create good karma without others, and enlightenment would be impossible! It is said in the teachings that all of our happiness, from basic essentials like water and food up to the highest happiness of enlightenment, comes to us from other beings. When we realize this, love and positive wishes for others will arise easily and spontaneously.

DEDICATION

When you are ready to conclude the meditation, dedicate the positive energy of your meditation to all beings, intently wishing that they find happiness and, ultimately, enlightenment.

A Loving-Kindness Meditation on Maitreya Buddha

This meditation involves visualizing Maitreya, the Buddha who embodies the quality of loving-kindness (his name derives from the Sanskrit word for loving-kindness, *maitri*). Maitreya is also said to be the next Buddha, who will teach the path to liberation and enlightenment after the teachings of Shakyamuni Buddha have disappeared from our world. As mentioned above, if you do not feel comfortable visualizing Maitreya Buddha, you can visualize another figure or image that represents loving-kindness. The purpose of the visualization is to get in touch with and develop love within our own heart. Simply replace the visualization described below with the image of your choice, and follow the remaining steps of the meditation.★

★Note: this is a slightly revised version of the "Maitreya Peace Meditation" that I composed in 2005 at the request of the Maitreya Project (an FPMT project to build a 500-foot statue of Maitreya in Kushinagar, India).

Maitreya

PREPARATION

Sit in a comfortable position, with your back straight, and take a few min-utes to relax your body and mind. Let your eyes close gently, and let your body become relaxed, light, and free from tension. Let your breath flow in and out in a natural rhythm.

Relax your mind by letting go of thoughts—thoughts of the past or the future, thoughts of your work, other places, or people. Let these thoughts drift out of your awareness, and decide to keep your mind in the present, focused on the meditation, without being distracted by anything else or wandering aimlessly away.

MOTIVATION

Generate a positive motivation for doing this meditation. For example, you can think that you are doing the meditation in order to have more love, kindness, and compassion in your heart to give to others and to the world. If you are comfortable with the idea, you can also think that you are doing it to become enlightened, to help all beings.

MAIN MEDITATION

Now visualize in the space in front of you a figure or image that represents absolute purity, goodness, peace, universal love, and compassion. This figure could be Maitreya, the embodiment of loving-kindness, or another Buddhist figure that you are familiar with. If you prefer, you can visualize a figure from Christianity such as Jesus, Mary, or one of the saints. Or it could be a figure from another religious tradition that you are familiar with and that represents for you these positive qualities. You could also simply visualize light: a sphere or beam of radiant white or golden light. The point is to think of a representation of pure love and compassion you are comfortable with, and imagine it in front of you. Visualize it as not solid, like our bodies, but made of light, transparent and radiant.

If you do wish to visualize Maitreya, imagine that his body is made of radiant golden light, and that his appearance is youthful, peaceful, and smiling. Don't be concerned about having a perfect, clear image. Just do the best you can, and be satisfied with that. The most important thing is to feel that it's really there; that you are sitting in the presence of this representation of goodness, perfection, purity, universal loving-kindness, and compassion. Spend some time getting a sense of the loving-kindness Maitreya feels for you and every other living being in the universe, without exception. His love does not discriminate people who are beautiful or ugly, wealthy or poor, intelligent or dull, well-mannered or unruly. He loves all beings equally, not because of their appearance or behavior, but just because they exist. He views all of us in the way a loving mother sees her small child: beautiful, precious, totally deserving of love. And his love is constant, not fleeting; he is there, ready to help us, every moment, hour, day, month, and year, forever. He is completely non-judgmental, and always forgives us, no matter what we do. Try to really feel this loving-kindness and compassion emanating from Maitreya to yourself and all other beings. Moreover, understand that you also have the capacity to develop such love.

Now visualize light streaming from your visualized image into you, and filling your body as if it were like an empty vase being filled with liquid. The light flows down to the tips of your toes and fingers. It then fills your legs, hands, arms, torso, neck, and head, right up to the top of your head. It fills every cell, atom, and tiny particle of your body. This light purifies all of your troubles and pain—physical pain and sickness, as well as mental unhappiness, negative thoughts, and the imprints of harmful actions you did in the past. Everything negative in your body and mind is completely cleansed, and disappears like the darkness in a room when the light is switched on.

Imagine that your body is suffused with blissful, radiant light, and becomes clean and clear like a piece of crystal. Imagine that your mind becomes calm and clear, free of all disturbing thoughts, and filled with feelings of loving-kindness and compassion. Imagine that you become inseparable from the image in front of you, the embodiment of loving-kindness and compassion. You yourself become just like that—totally positive, loving, compassionate, peaceful, and blissful. Let your mind rest in this experience for a few minutes, without thinking of anything else.

Now generate the wish to share this peaceful, loving energy with others, so that they too may become free from suffering, and filled with positive energy. Imagine the energy of loving-kindness radiating out from your heart to all directions like rays of light emanating from the sun. Imagine that it first touches other people who are in the room with you, or in the house or building you are in. Imagine that they become filled with the energy of loving-kindness.

Then send it out further to all the people in your *neighborhood*. They all become filled with this light of loving-kindness. Send it out further to all the people in your *town or city*, and imagine that they all become filled with the energy of loving-kindness. Continue, sending the light out to the people in *other countries*, so that gradually all people in *all countries in the world* become filled with loving-kindness. Imagine sending it out to other beings as well: non-human beings such as animals, birds, fish and marine life, and insects—*all living beings*, everywhere in the world. They all become filled with the energy of loving-kindness.

Imagine sending it out to all the beings in the universe; imagine that all of them become filled with loving-kindness. The minds of all beings everywhere become free of negative thoughts, and filled with loving thoughts, so that now there is peace everywhere. Then spend some time sitting quietly with whatever feelings are present in your mind.

Dedication

When you are ready to conclude the meditation, dedicate the positive energy you created, sincerely wishing that it will bring peace to all beings, everywhere. For example, you can think or say, "May all beings everywhere become free from suffering. May their minds be free of all thoughts of intolerance, anger, hatred, and the wish to give harm. May their minds be filled instead with patience, respect, loving-kindness, and the wish only to benefit others. May they all be happy." You can also dedicate the merit you have developed to all beings with the wish that they may ultimately attain enlightenment, the highest state of happiness.

4

Immeasurable Compassion

May all beings be free from suffering and the causes of suffering.

Compassion arises out of our own experience of suffering. We all know what it's like to be sick or in pain, to be lonely or have our feelings hurt by an unkind remark, to fear the unknown or grieve the death of a loved one. When we then see or hear of others going through similar experiences, our heart opens with a feeling of empathy and the wish to help. This is compassion—the wish for oneself and others to be free of suffering, free from all painful, unwanted, unsatisfactory experiences. It acknowledges that *everyone* wants to be free of suffering, deserves to be free, and has the capacity to be free.

It's a quality we already have—an innate aspect of everyone's mind—but in most of us it is limited. We feel it for some beings, but not for others; we feel it sometimes but not always. We have the capacity, however, to feel compassion for everyone, all of the time—immeasurable compassion. By making our mind increasingly familiar with the right thoughts and feelings, our compassion will gradually increase and eventually become immeasurable.

Compassion differs slightly from love—what we've been calling "loving-kindness" in the previous chapters. Love wants others *to be happy*, while compassion wants them *to not suffer*. Love comes from appreciating others' kindness, or just respecting them as fellow beings, whereas compassion comes from realizing that they suffer. Love and compassion are like two sides of a coin: when we love others, we naturally want them to not suffer, and when we have compassion for others, we naturally want them to be happy. They both focus on beings but in different ways, and there are different methods for developing them.

Avoiding Denial and Despair

Since developing compassion depends on being aware of suffering, it's essential that our attitudes about suffering are healthy and realistic. There are two attitudes we might have that are *not* healthy and realistic. One of these is denial, not wanting to acknowledge the existence of the unpleasant, unwanted aspects of life. I had this attitude when I was young. I received my first Buddhist teaching when I was at university in California, from a woman I met who was a disciple of Zen master Suzuki Roshi. I was interested in Buddhism and asked her to tell me something about it. We got together one day, and she began to explain the Four Noble Truths. When she talked about the First Noble Truth, that life is suffering, I protested, "How can you say that? Life is beautiful!" She looked straight in my eyes and calmly said, "I can see that you are suffering." I was dumbfounded; it was as if she had thrown a glass of cold water in my face. She was right—most of my life I had been deeply unhappy, even suicidal at times—but I did I not want to accept it.

Why do we deny suffering? Different people deny their suffering for different reasons and in different ways. In my own case, I desperately wanted to be a happy person, and thought that if I ignored my problems and pretended everything was fine, the problems would simply go away. Another reason could be shame. Admitting that you are not happy—that you are not like the ecstatic-looking people in cigarette and alcohol advertisements—is admitting that something is wrong with you, that you are a failure. Fear could be another factor: we think that if we accept and open to suffering, it will overwhelm us like a tsunami, and any happiness we have will be washed away forever.

Yet another reason could be that we simply don't know any other way to be. Methods for learning to acknowledge and deal skillfully with suffering are not readily available in our culture. And we don't have many role models, examples of people who are doing it. The norm is to avoid and run away. There are so many escape routes available: drugs and alcohol, entertainment, sports, work, food, sleep, shopping, socializing. It's so much easier to turn to one of these—as yet another form of denial— than to sit down, face our problems, and find constructive ways of solving them.

Another unhealthy attitude about suffering is despair, the opposite of denial. It happens when we open our hearts to suffering, but let ourselves be overpowered by the immensity of it: there is just so much of it, and so little we can do. We then feel depressed and hopeless, and may even shut down: "I don't want to hear about any more suffering; I can't take it." I have heard that the word "compassion" has a negative connotation to some people, and this may be the reason: they think that being compassionate means being miserable, and the more compassion you have the more miserable you are!

This is not the meaning of compassion in Buddhism. Just look at the Dalai Lama, one of the most compassionate people on the planet—does he look miserable? Most of the time he is glowing with joyful energy, smiling, laughing, and joking. He's not denying suffering nor is he wallowing in despair. He has been carrying on his shoulders the enormous problems of Tibet since he was a teenager. And for decades he has been traveling all over the world, meeting many different people, from politicians to scientists to ordinary folks, and learning about the problems of countries other than his own. He has certainly opened his mind and heart to the suffering of the world, but is not the least bit depressed about it. He explains that when facing a problem, there may be for a short time some turmoil in the intellectual side of his mind—thinking about the problem and experiencing some worry—but the emotional side remains calm, like the depths of the ocean. There is a poem by the Dalai Lama that many people have hung on their walls that begins:

Never give up.
No matter what is going on,
Never give up.

Develop the heart...
Be compassionate...

This approach suggests the kind of healthy attitude we can develop about suffering.

Accepting Suffering

A more positive, constructive approach to suffering is one that could be thought of as the middle way between the two extremes of denial and despair. This involves accepting the existence of suffering on one hand, while on the other hand dealing with it in an optimistic, practical way. Despair and hopelessness are useless and debilitating; they leave us with little or no positive energy to give to others or to use to find a workable solution. Genuine compassion is aware of the suffering of others, and wants them to be free of it, but instead of being despondent, it is optimistic and energetic. This is because it is balanced with insight into the real nature of suffering, which enables us to deal with it in a healthy way.

So how can we develop this more healthy attitude toward suffering? Here are some perspectives from the Buddhist teachings that can help us.

SUFFERING IS A REALITY.

This is the first of the Buddha's Four Noble Truths. It is simply the nature of samsara/cyclic existence—the situation we are in as long as we have not attained liberation or enlightenment—to be imperfect, unsatisfactory, and full of problems. Suffering and problems are a natural, inevitable part of everyone's life. It is sensible to adopt the attitude of expecting that they will happen, and accepting them when they do. They won't go away simply by denying them, looking the other way, or pretending they're not there.

SUFFERING IS NOT PERMANENT.

It won't be there forever. It does not exist independently but arises from causes and conditions, which are also not permanent. As we have seen, the root of suffering is ignorance, seeing ourselves and everyone and everything else in mistaken ways: as real, permanent, and existing independently. And here we go again, on the samsaric wheel: ignorance gives rise to other delusions like anger and attachment, and under the control of these mental states, we create the actions or karma that result in unpleasant, painful experiences. Once we understand how this process works, we can see that suffering is not a permanent condition.

SUFFERING IS NOT NECESSARILY A BAD THING.

Going through difficult, unwanted experiences does not have to be terrible or unbearable. Problems can be opportunities for learning and growth; they can even be beautiful and inspiring. A friend who had cancer when he was just in his twenties said it was the best thing that ever happened to him. Through that experience, he resolved old problems with his family and developed closer ties with them. He also became interested in the spiritual path, learned meditation, and even decided to become a monk so he could devote himself fulltime to spiritual study and practice. There are many cases of people who have made constructive changes in their lives after going through a difficult time.

The Indian master Santideva pointed out a number of benefits of suffering in his text *A Guide to the Bodhisattva's Way of Life*, one of the most widely used and profound guides to developing compassion. Suffering, Shantideva says, makes us more humble and less arrogant. It enables us to feel compassion for other beings who are suffering. We will be more motivated to act positively and avoid negative actions, because we realize that it is our actions that cause the experiences we have, good and bad. And we will have greater disillusionment with samsara and aspire to follow the path to freedom. Problems can be terrible or beneficial, then, depending on how we look at and deal with them. In chapter 8 we will look at some methods for transforming problems into opportunities for spiritual practice.

WE CAN BE PRACTICAL—EVEN IN A CRISIS.

Another verse from Santideva's text gives very useful advice on what to do when there's a problem or crisis: "Why be unhappy about something if it can be remedied? And what is the use of being unhappy about something if it cannot be remedied?" In other words, if there is something we can do to prevent or remedy a painful or unwanted situation, we should do it. On the other hand, if there's nothing we can do, it's useless to worry or be unhappy; we should simply accept it. Acceptance doesn't mean denial or running away. It means fully acknowledging the painful situation, but also acknowledging our limitations: that we cannot do anything about it.

For example, when someone is injured or in pain, we do what we can to get proper medical help, pain medication, and whatever is necessary for the person to be as comfortable as possible. We can also talk to her, find out any worries or concerns she may have, and do our best to take care of those. If, in spite of all our efforts, the person still experiences physical or mental suffering, we simply have to accept that. We have done all we can. Being upset, anxious, or sad is of no use to anyone. If you believe in prayer, you can always do that, and of course you can do any of the meditations we are learning about in this book. Even these are practical methods that can bring calm and warmth rather than anxiety to a very difficult situation.

One of my teachers, Denma Locho Rinpoche, told a story of how he used Santideva's advice to deal with a crisis. He said that he didn't face many problems in his life, despite escaping from Tibet in 1959 because of the Communist occupation, and becoming a refugee in India. But there was one occasion when his mind become so upset that it was difficult to continue his study and practice: that was during the Cultural Revolution of the sixties, when he heard about the violence and destruction the Chinese were carrying out in Tibet. Remembering this verse from Santideva's text enabled him to realize the uselessness of being upset about something he could not change, and to restore his mind to a balanced state.

SENTIENT BEINGS ARE RESPONSIBLE FOR THEIR OWN SUFFERING.

We sometimes think it is our responsibility to solve other people's problems or remove their suffering, and then we feel guilty if we are unable to do so. In reality, the root causes of suffering are the delusions and karma within beings' minds, and only they are able to eliminate these. No one can do it for them, not even an enlightened being. The Buddha once said:

> Buddhas do not wash away negativities with water,
> They do not clear away beings' suffering with their hands,
> They do not transfer their own knowledge to others;
> They liberate by teaching the truth of reality.

If even buddhas are unable to remove others' suffering, or give them happiness and realizations, then we certainly cannot do so! Therefore, generating compassion does not mean actually freeing beings from their suffering; it is *wishing* that they be free. Of course, if there are things we can do to help, we should do them. Sometimes our efforts will work, sometimes not. The most skilled doctor is unable to cure every patient, and the most courageous rescue worker can't save every life. No matter how strongly we may wish someone to be free from a problem, we may not be able to bring this about. We can only try our best, and then accept whatever the result may be.

These reminders can be used to encourage us to develop a more balanced and beneficial attitude toward suffering so that we can generate compassion and work to help others without succumbing to depression or burn-out. Sakya Trizin Rinpoche, the head of the Sakya tradition of Tibetan Buddhism, was once asked by a student how a bodhisattva can open his or her heart to all the suffering of all beings and not become depressed about it. He replied that the way a bodhisattva deals with the suffering of beings is similar to the way we would deal with a friend who is asleep and having a nightmare, tossing and turning in his sleep, crying out. Although we feel compassion for our friend and want to help him, we do not feel upset because we know that what he is experiencing is happening in his mind. So we simply wake him up and reassure him that it was only a dream. Similarly, bodhisattvas, through their wisdom of the true nature of things, are aware of the suffering of beings but know that it is not real, permanent, and independently existing. Thus they are not upset about it, but simply work to help beings wake up from the sleep of ignorance and attain the wisdom that will free them, once and for all, from suffering.

Bodhisattvas are practical. They do what they can to help beings, but knowing they cannot eliminate all suffering right now, they also strive for enlightenment. Once they have attained that state, they will be able to help all beings in the best possible way, without any limitation.

The Benefits of Cultivating Compassion

We will be more inspired to cultivate compassion if we understand the benefits of doing so. I have not seen a concise list of the benefits of compassion, as there is for loving-kindness, but a number of texts say that compassion is important in the beginning, middle, and end of the bodhisattvas' path. It is important at the beginning in order to generate bodhichitta, the aspiration to become enlightened for the benefit of others; it is important in the middle in order to practice the bodhisattvas' deeds that benefit others and create the causes for enlightenment; and it is important at the end, once enlightenment has been attained, in order to carry out the welfare of all beings.

For those of us who are not yet bodhisattvas, there are benefits we can begin to experience even now. For one thing, compassion is an exquisitely wonderful state of mind to experience. As a teenager, I was so moved by a speech given by Portia in Shakespeare's *Merchant of Venice* that I still remember it today:

> The quality of mercy is not strained.
> It droppeth like the gentle rain from heaven upon the place
> beneath.
> It is twice blest; it blesseth he that gives, and he that
> receives....

As she says, we are truly "blessed" when we can feel compassion, or mercy. It makes our heart soft, gentle, caring, and open. It enables us to feel connected to others, and thus less lonely and fearful. It inspires us to reach out and offer a helping hand, or to just sit quietly, lovingly, in the presence of someone who is in pain. Compassion makes us feel good, so it's an effective remedy for unhappiness and depression. Research shows that being kind and helpful to others makes us more happy—it causes our body to release endorphins, the "happy hormones"—and also strengthens our immune system. So compassion is good for our mind and our body!

Compassion itself is a positive state that immediately benefits our mind, but it also motivates us to do positive actions, which are helpful both to ourselves and others. It is the basis for *giving*, one of the most important practices in all religious traditions. Giving is practiced because there are beings who are in need, and giving them what they need relieves their suffering. It also benefits us. It expands our heart, enables us to express our compassion, and creates the causes for happiness in the future: good rebirths, always having what we need, and, ultimately, enlightenment.

Giving is one of the six perfections, the principal practices of bodhisattvas (the other five are ethics, patience, joyous effort, concentration, and wisdom). There are several types of giving we can practice: we can give resources such as money and food, protection from fear and danger, love, and spiritual advice and teachings when appropriate. Ideally, giving should be done with an altruistic motivation rather than the wish to receive something in return, or to be admired by others. Cultivating compassion therefore enables us to practice giving with the proper attitude.

Compassion also stops us from harming others. As we noted in the loving-kindness meditation on the kindness of others, *ethics* is the practice of refraining from harmful actions. For example, when we see a cockroach in our kitchen, our first impulse might be to squash it out of existence. But we can stop and think, "This is a being who, because of unskillful karma, has been born in this unfortunate situation, living in sewers, eating garbage, trying to avoid being stepped on or sprayed with poison. It wants to stay alive as much as I do." With this understanding, we choose to not kill it. (Of course, we don't have to let it stay in our kitchen—we can catch it and take it outside.) By living our life in a compassionate and non-violent way as much as possible, other beings are safe from being harmed by us, and that itself is doing them a great service.

Refraining from harming others is also beneficial for ourselves. When we intentionally kill or injure another being, say hurtful words, or just think negative thoughts about someone, we hurt not only others but ourselves as well. It is impossible to be truly, deeply happy when we engage in destructive behavior. We might feel a few moments of delight that we got back at someone who hurt us, or asserted our dominant role, but deep down inside we *know* that we did something wrong. People who have near-death experiences confirm this: they sometimes see their entire life flash by in a few moments, remembering all the hurtful things they ever did, as well as *feeling* the suffering of those they hurt.

When I was first studying Buddhism in Dharamsala, I once saw my teacher at that time, Geshe Ngawang Dhargyey, bend down and pick up a worm from a path and gently place it on the side of the path so it would not be stepped on. I was amazed. Coming from a culture where insects are regarded as repulsive pests to be exterminated, I felt deeply touched by this gesture of kindness and compassion. Even more impressive was the fact that the person who did this was a highly learned and respected lama who had many disciples. Nevertheless, he was humble enough to save a small insect from danger. I also heard of a Zen monk who put a mosquito net around his bed, not to keep the mosquitoes from biting him, but to make sure that he did not harm *them* while he slept. By practicing compassion we can thus make a remarkable change in our attitude: from wishing to kill insects in order to protect ourselves, to feeling responsible to protect them from harm.

Compassion also helps us to practice *patience*. There are different kinds of patience; one is learning to not become angry and retaliate when someone harms us. This kind of patience can be practiced simply by understanding the faults of anger and the benefits of patience. However, conjoining our practice with compassion enhances and strengthens our patience. It helps us realize that someone who harms us is already suffering himself; getting angry and retaliating will just add to his suffering, and our compassion doesn't want to do that, but wants to help him instead.

Another benefit of compassion is that it helps us to *forgive*. Forgiveness is a beautiful, healing quality, but it is sometimes difficult to generate. We cling to the past as if it's still existing today; we see those who wronged us as inherently, permanently bad, and undeserving of our love and compassion. Worst of all, we don't realize we are actually hurting ourselves with these attitudes; we may even think we're doing the right thing.

Our inability to forgive others may stem from our inability to forgive ourselves. Not forgiving ourselves involves identifying with our mistakes or harmful actions, because we think we are permanent ("I am exactly the same person who did those awful things twenty years ago"). It may also involve guilt, self-hatred, and feeling that we don't deserve to be happy, but deserve to suffer. It's as though we give ourselves a life sentence without parole in a mental prison of misery. If we condemn ourselves like this, it's only natural that we will do the same to others. The solution is to realize that these attitudes are unwise and to change them. We need to realize that there is no permanent, concrete "bad" person in our body-mind complex. We are simply a being who, due to ignorance, delusions, and karma sometimes acts unskillfully, but that is not our real nature—which is pure, free of negative thoughts and tendencies. The Buddhist alternative to guilt and self-blame is to feel *regret* for our unskillful actions, try our best to avoid repeating them, and make up for them in whatever way we can. There are also practices that can be done to purify our negative karma. Through these methods we can learn to forgive ourselves, and then we will find it easier to forgive others.

Finally, we can appreciate the importance of compassion by imagining what the world would be like without it. A natural disaster like an earthquake would happen, and no one would help the victims. Nobody would take care of those who are sick, dying, impoverished, homeless, mentally ill, or disabled—these people would be left to fend for themselves. Unfortunately, this does sometimes happen, but don't we feel outraged about it? And don't we feel moved when we hear of efforts to relieve suffering, and want to contribute to them? This shows that we *do* recognize the value of compassion, and would like to see more of it in the world, and in ourselves. And this can be achieved, by using the methods for cultivating a kind, caring heart.

Suffering and Its Causes

Since cultivating compassion involves generating the wish for beings to be free of suffering and its causes, what *kind* of suffering do we wish them to not have? We can begin by thinking about the painful experiences that are easy to recognize: war, terrorism, violent crime, hunger, physical and mental illness, injustice, abuse, natural disasters, drought and famine, drug and alcohol addiction, and so on. The Buddhist teachings delineate numerous examples of sufferings, including some we would never have thought of. In his first teaching, on the Four Noble Truths, Buddha gave a list of afflictions that humans and other beings experience in the course of their lives: birth, aging, sickness, death, sorrow, lamentation, pain, grief, despair, encountering what is unpleasant, having to separate from what is pleasant, not getting what we want, and simply having a body-mind complex that is subject to painful experiences.

In addition to these examples of sufferings that are relatively easy to identify, there are others that are more subtle. Contemplating these will make our compassion deeper and more extensive. One way to do this is by reflecting on the *three kinds of suffering*, which include all the problems in samsara.

THE SUFFERING OF SUFFERING

This refers to experiences that are clearly unpleasant and unsatisfactory, such as those mentioned above, as well as normal everyday problems like physical aches and pains, hunger and thirst, feeling too hot or cold, being bored or restless, lonely or sad, and so forth.

THE SUFFERING OF CHANGE

This level of suffering is more subtle and difficult to recognize. It refers to the experiences we normally think of as pleasure or happiness. Buddhism considers that ordinary pleasure is not true happiness, but just another kind of suffering, because it does not last or provide long-term satisfaction, and does not free us from our problems. Consider eating. The pleasure we derive is fleeting, and if we eat too much, it becomes suffering rather than pleasure. Even then, after a few hours we feel hungry again. A great deal of time and energy goes into buying and preparing food, and cleaning up afterward, not to mention working to earn money to be able to buy food in the first place—all that effort for just a small amount of pleasure. Of course we must eat to stay alive, but the point here is to question the concept of eating being a source of genuine happiness. The same applies to other "pleasant" experiences such as playing sports, having sex, sleeping, entertainment, and so on. If we examine them objectively, it is difficult to find any real, lasting pleasure or happiness.

PERVASIVE SUFFERING

This is an even more subtle level of suffering. It refers to our very existence in samsara, which is due to our mind being under the control of delusions and karma. Although our mind is clear and pure by nature, it is temporarily obscured by ignorance, other delusions, and the imprints of our past actions. Because of these, we experience all the various problems of life, and have to die and be reborn again and again. Being in samsara is like being in a prison, not free to enjoy the peace and happiness of liberation and enlightenment.

We can get an idea of this third kind of suffering by trying to keep our mind focused for a few minutes on a positive thought, such as wishing all beings to be happy. What happens? Can we keep our mind concentrated on this thought, or are there other thoughts that keep intruding? Are some of these other thoughts negative? Thoughts that you would prefer not to have?

Just as we are unable to control our mind for even a few minutes, we are unable to control our life. We wish to always have pleasant, positive experiences, but are we able to? Is it not the case that unwanted experiences and events occur over and over again? And we probably want to be a good person, kind and helpful to others, but is this always possible, or do we sometimes find ourselves saying and doing nasty things, almost as if we are possessed by a demon? Taking a good, honest look at our life and our mind makes it clear that we are not really free and in control of our thoughts, actions, and experiences. We call this suffering "pervasive" because it pervades the whole of samsara: every experience in the life of every samsaric being is imperfect and unsatisfying.

Awareness of the more subtle forms of suffering makes us realize that all beings deserve compassion, even those who seem to have everything, and even those who cause suffering to others—perpetrators of violence, abuse, and injustice. These are probably the most difficult people to feel compassion for, but they suffer too. This becomes clear when we put ourselves in their place and try to understand why they behave the way they do. Their minds are overrun by negative states: anger, greed, selfishness, pride, ignorance, fear, and confusion. They are not happy, peaceful human beings; they are in a mental hell, tormented by delusions. In addition, the karma they are creating will cause them to experience even more suffering in the future, probably for many lifetimes, before they become free.

It is also helpful to mentally separate people and the delusions in their mind. As mentioned before, negative thoughts and emotions are not permanent aspects of our being, and they are not who we are. They are transient mental states that come and go in our mind, but never damage the innate purity of our mind. Lama Yeshe said that thoughts are like tourists who stay in a place just for a short time, whereas the pure nature of the mind is like a permanent resident. So even the most cruel, harmful people who create an enormous amount of pain and destruction are not that way permanently; that is not their real nature. They behave that way only temporarily, because of causes and conditions—mainly the presence of strong delusions in their mind—but like all beings they have buddha nature, and one day they will be enlightened beings, free of all negativity and perfect in all positive qualities, working to help all other beings.

It may be difficult initially to accept some of these ideas, so take time to think about them. Making our minds more familiar with them will enable us to feel less angry toward destructive people, and recognize that they too deserve compassion.

Compassion wishes all beings to be free not only from suffering but also from its *causes*: delusions and unskillful karma. These are the factors that keep us locked in the prison of samsara and produce all the painful experiences we encounter. Thus when we meditate on compassion, we should wish ourselves and others to be free not only from suffering but also from negative attitudes such as hatred, greed, and ignorance, and from negative actions such as killing, stealing, and lying. In this way we will avoid creating the causes to suffer in the future.

Although contemplating the many varieties of suffering broadens your experience of compassion, you should do so in a balanced way, to avoid being overwhelmed and possibly sinking into despair. Do what is manageable. You might find it effective to start with yourself—learning to be more aware and accepting of your own problems will make it easier to recognize those of others. Then slowly open up to the sufferings of the people around you: those you live, work, and interact with every day. There are people in need all around us—in our family, neighborhood, workplace, and community. Opening our heart to their problems and doing what we can to help them is an ideal way to cultivate and practice compassion. When you have gained greater familiarity with the more obvious forms of suffering, you can gradually move on to contemplate the subtler forms: the suffering of change and pervasive suffering, the dissatisfaction of all beings everywhere.

Obstacles to Compassion

In addition to the two unhealthy attitudes about suffering mentioned above—denial and despair—there are several other mental states that can hinder our cultivation of compassion.

One of these is *cruelty*, the very opposite of compassion: the desire to give harm or to see someone suffer. We feel horrified when we hear accounts of torture, and wonder how a human being could be so cruel to other people. But it we carefully observe our mind, we may notice similar thoughts. When we are very angry at someone, especially if that person has deeply wounded us, we may have thoughts of saying or doing something unkind to hurt the person as badly as he hurt us. Or if such a person experiences misfortune, we may secretly feel glad: "Good, you deserve it." So if we are honest, we may discover that we too have cruelty. And it is important to be honest because if this attitude goes unnoticed and unremedied, it might reveal itself one day in some deplorable way.

What can we do about cruelty? Since it is based on anger and hatred, working on overcoming those mental states will counteract it. Furthermore, cultivating thoughts of loving-kindness and compassion—wishing others to be happy and to *not* suffer—will diminish the likelihood that malicious thoughts would arise in our mind and, even if they do, that we would act them out. It's also helpful to remember that whatever thoughts arise in our mind are cloud-like, transitory phenomena passing through our mind, so we can choose to ignore and not identify with them.

Another obstacle is *pity*. This state of mind is similar to compassion, but while compassion is positive and balanced, pity includes some unskillful attitudes, like fear. Seeing another's suffering brings up the worry that it might happen to us as well, and we can't bear the thought, so we don't want to get too close or stay too long. We pay a visit to our sick friend in the hospital, but stay only a few minutes, saying we're sorry but we have to get back to work. We toss a coin in the homeless person's cup, trying to avoid looking in his eyes, and quickly walk off. While chatting with a friend, she mentions a natural disaster that just occurred, and we say, "How awful!" then immediately change the subject. This is pity, not compassion.

Pity is also condescending: it has a sense of our being above and beyond the suffering of the pathetic beings beneath us. Compassion is not like that. It is based on realistic ways of thinking. It understands that suffering is not permanent or independently existing, that it can be eliminated, and that we are all in the same situation in samsara. No being, including oneself, is beyond suffering. With such understanding, we are less fearful about being in the presence of suffering, and we feel equal rather than superior to others because we know that their suffering could be ours.

Cynicism is another attitude that can obstruct compassion. The Dalai Lama often expresses his belief that human beings are by nature loving and compassionate, but some Western people find that difficult to accept. The news each day is filled with accounts of war, violence, terrorism, injustice, greed, and corruption. It's easy to think that people are naturally selfish and cruel rather than kind and caring, and that there is no way we can change. Such a cynical view of human nature could lead us to think that it's pointless to even try to cultivate loving-kindness and compassion.

Consider this: the vast majority of interactions that take place every moment of every day between the almost seven billion or so human beings on this planet are peaceful and nonviolent. People work together, sit together on trains, buses, and airplanes, walk past each other in the streets and shopping malls, and share living space, all without harming each other. Moreover, billions of these relations between people are loving and kind: family members and friends care for one another and help each other with difficulties; doctors, nurses, psychologists, and social workers look after those who are suffering; aid organizations provide for the needs of refugees, and so forth. The incidence of people killing and harming each other is comparatively small. That is why such stories are reported in the news: because they are atypical. They are also sensational; they are what people *want* to hear. But focusing only on these stories and overlooking the everyday activities of ordinary people leads to a pessimistic, cynical picture of humanity.

When reading newspapers or watching news on TV, we need to be careful to avoid despair and cynicism. Of course, hostility and fighting do exist, but they are the exception rather than the norm. Open your eyes and ears; pay attention to the people around you, what they are doing and how they are behaving, and you will observe that there is far more kindness and compassion than violence.

Compassion in Daily Life

It's a good idea to spend at least a few minutes each day, preferably in the morning, reflecting on the fact that beings want to be happy and free from suffering, just as you do, and generating loving-kindness and compassion for them. Remember these thoughts during the day as well, especially when you are among people—at work or school, walking through a crowd on the street or in a shopping mall. If you can deeply habituate your mind to this truth, it will help you be more kind and considerate. It's particularly useful to remember these ideas when you find yourself feeling judgmental, impatient, or irritated toward anyone. Think, "This person just wants to be happy, and does not want suffering." Your perception of the person will shift in a more positive direction.

Use your own problems to remember that others have problems too, and wish to be free from them. Let's say you feel stressed or bored with your life. Say to yourself, "I'm not the only person in the world with a stressful or boring life. There are many others with jobs and lives just as boring and stressful as mine, or even more so." Contemplate that other people, with problems like yours or worse, want to be free from the suffering of unpleasant work, or of joblessness, then generate the compassionate wish that they could be free from this and all other suffering, as well as the causes of suffering. Not only does this increase our compassion, it also makes our own "problems" appear more manageable.

Once again, in bringing compassion to everyday life it's helpful to remember the limitations we discussed. You can't literally remove people's deep suffering. True compassion is loving-concern balanced with clear wisdom. Wisdom enables us to stay calm and think clearly of how best to help. For example, if someone in our family suddenly becomes ill or has an accident, we are able to put aside fear, worry, and self-concern, and swiftly do what needs to be done.

When it comes to helping someone who is suffering mentally, greater wisdom and skill are required. It's easy to get distracted by someone's drama and drawn into it and lose sight of the means to act compassionately. Let's say a friend comes to see us, upset because his girlfriend has just rejected him. With compassion we listen to his outpouring of grief and anger, empathize with what he's going through, and offer kind words to console him. But it's not wise to think that we must solve his problem for him, or to become as depressed and angry as he is. Instead, we should use our wisdom and skillful means to help him come to terms with his problem. For example, we can explain to him that being angry is not helpful, but only increases his suffering. And doing something to hurt his girlfriend might make him feel good for a few minutes, but will just cause more problems in the long run. We can advise him to try to work things out with his girlfriend, but if it looks like the break is irreparable, it's best for him to accept what has happened, forgive and forget, and get on with his life. Throughout our conversation, we can remain calm, show our concern by listening attentively, avoid preaching or giving unwanted advice, and think clearly how best to help him work out his own solution to the problem. If we can balance compassion with wisdom in this way, he will feel better and we will be able to walk away without carrying his problem on our shoulders.

In order to have compassion toward someone who harms us or our loved ones we can imagine ourselves in his shoes: "What is he thinking? How does he feel? What makes him behave like this?" If we do this with an open heart, we'll realize that he's suffering, not happy, and that his mind is possessed by delusions, like someone suffering from a psychological disorder. By understanding this, we realize that it's more appropriate to respond with calm patience instead of anger and retaliation.

Being compassionate, though, doesn't mean letting the person continue to act aggressively. We should do what we can to protect ourselves and others from harm, but with compassion—rather than hatred—in our heart. Also, we should try to ensure that our actions are ethical and non-harmful. There are a number of non-violent alternatives we can try: prevention, dialogue, or seeking help from those with greater authority and skill. Also, living a life of compassion and non-violence reduces the likelihood of finding ourselves in threatening, dangerous situations in the first place, unless we have consciously chosen to enter them in order to act compassionately.

Being compassionate also does not mean saying "yes" every time we are asked to give or do something. It's okay to say "no" if we feel that the request is inappropriate or non-beneficial; for example, a child asking for lots of toys and sweets, or an addict asking for money to buy drugs. We can also say "no" if we are incapable of fulfilling the request, or if we feel the person is trying to use us for her own selfish ends.

Some people think it's cowardly to react to aggression with patience and compassion, but it actually takes a great deal of courage to respond nonviolently. Practicing compassion rather than violence can bring powerful and far-reaching consequences. Shakyamuni Buddha countered the negative forces that tried to disturb his final meditation with loving-kindness, and through that was able to attain enlightenment. Jesus Christ compassionately forgave the men who abused and killed him, and his example has become a profound source of inspiration for billions of people around the world. Mahatma Gandhi and his followers won India's independence through nonviolent activities, even at the risk of death or imprisonment. Meeting harm and injustice with compassionate nonviolence is far more noble and courageous than fighting back.

5
Meditations for Cultivating Compassion

As long as space remains
As long as beings remain
Until then may I too remain
And dispel the miseries of the world.
—Shantideva

The most well-known traditional meditation for cultivating compassion involves contemplating the suffering that others are experiencing and their desire to be free of it, and then generating the wish that they be free. The first meditation here is based on that principle. The second meditation is similar to the meditation on Maitreya Buddha. In this case, we meditate on the Buddha of Compassion. Visualizing an embodied form can help to make our meditation less abstract, so meditations on Chenrezig (in Tibetan; or Avalokiteshvara in Sanskrit; Kuan-Yin or Guanyin in Chinese; and Kanzeon or Kannon in Japanese) are some of the most widely practiced means for developing a compassionate heart. Another excellent meditation related to compassion, "taking and giving" (*tong-len*) is explained in section two, under verse 7.

Meditation on Compassion

As with the meditation on loving-kindness, it is most effective to first develop compassion for individuals, one person at a time, then gradually extend it to more and more beings, and finally to all beings. The usual sequence is to begin with someone who you know is suffering, then move on to a friend, a neutral person, an "enemy," and all beings. However, I placed a meditation on compassion for oneself at the beginning, because it is said in the teachings that we cannot really develop compassion for others if we do not understand our own suffering and feel the wish to be free of it.

Spend as much time as you like on each part of the practice, and do as many parts as you wish in each session. The explanation of the meditation mentions only the suffering that each person is experiencing at present, but you may also like to contemplate other forms of suffering as explained in the previous chapter. For example, you can think of problems people will experience in the future as they age and die; the suffering of change (their pleasant experiences, which are not stable and long-lasting); and pervasive suffering (their very existence in samsara, controlled by delusions and karma). Feel free to bring to mind as many examples of unpleasant experiences as you want, and generate the heartfelt wish for the person to be free of them. You can also imagine the person *becoming* free of his or her suffering, and becoming peaceful, happy, and radiant.

As with the meditation on loving-kindness, you can repeat phrases to generate the feeling of compassion. You can use the phrases suggested below, or create your own. It is best to repeat the phrases a number of times, pausing between repetitions to let the words resonate in your heart.

If at any point in the meditation feelings of fear, depression, or despair arise in your mind, take note of these; don't deny them or try to push them away. As a remedy, remind yourself that suffering is not permanent. It occurs due to causes and conditions, it changes, and it will cease at some point. The situation is not hopeless, because there are practical methods for overcoming suffering and its causes. Remember as well that every being has the potential to be free forever of all suffering and its causes, and the potential to become blissfully enlightened.

PREPARATION

Sit comfortably with your back straight. Relax your body and let any tension dissolve and flow away. Spend a few minutes calming and settling your mind in the present moment, letting go of all other thoughts.

MOTIVATION

When your mind is calm and settled in the here and now, generate a positive, altruistic motivation for doing the meditation. You can think, for example, "May this meditation help me to increase my compassion so that I can make my life more beneficial for others and the world," or "May this meditation bring me closer to enlightenment so that I can help all other beings to be free of suffering and to attain enlightenment as well."

MAIN MEDITATION

Compassion for yourself
Begin by going into your heart and getting in touch with your wish to be happy and free of suffering. It is like a small voice inside that says, "I just want to be happy, and I don't want to have problems, unhappiness, or pain." This is something you share with all beings; everyone feels this way. And do not think that it is wrong to feel this way; you and everyone else *should* be happy and free of pain. It is our right as living beings.

Then bring to mind examples of your past and present suffering: physical problems such as illnesses, disabilities, aches and pains, being hot or cold, hunger and thirst, tiredness and tension; emotional problems such as fear, loneliness, grief, sadness, boredom; relationship problems; livelihood problems; financial problems; and so on.

Generate the wish to be free of all these problems: "May I be free of all physical suffering. May I be free of all mental suffering. May I be free of the causes of suffering." Repeat these phrases a number of times, pausing between repetitions to allow the feeling of compassion to grow within you. Remember that the causes of suffering are delusions—anger, attachment, and ignorance, the very root of all problems—and unskillful actions motivated by delusions. Wish that your mind may become liberated from these, like the sky free of clouds. Imagine yourself in this state of freedom: peaceful, joyful, and full of positive energy to benefit others and the world.

Compassion for someone who is suffering

Bring to mind a person or being you know who is suffering. You might choose someone who is easy to be concerned about, such as a child in pain or a small kitten or puppy crying for its mother. Or you might want to try a more difficult object, such as a person suffering from cancer or depression. The point is to develop the feeling of compassion without becoming overwhelmed by fear or despair. It is best to visualize the person in front of you or where she is right now, and spend some time contemplating the physical and/or mental pain she is experiencing. Contemplate that this person, just like you, wants to be free of suffering, and feel that she *deserves* to be free. Then generate the wish for her to be free. You can do this by saying to yourself phrases such as, "May you be free of all physical suffering. May you be free of all mental suffering. May you be free of the causes of suffering." If you find it helpful, visualize the person becoming free of her suffering and attaining a state of peace and happiness.

However, since it is possible that the person's suffering might not immediately disappear, you can also generate the wish that she finds the peace and strength needed to *accept* her suffering, and that the difficulties she is going through will enable her to develop wisdom, compassion, and other positive qualities.

Compassion for a friend

Think of someone you care about—a parent, another relative, or a dear friend. Visualize the person in front of you, or think of him where he is

right now—at home, at work, in a nursing home. Contemplate the physical and mental suffering he is experiencing now. Contemplate that he
wants to be free of this suffering, and feel that he deserves to be free.
Then generate the wish for him to be free. You can repeat the following
phrases, or whatever words you find helpful to generate compassion: "May
you be free of all physical suffering. May you be free of all mental suffering. May you be free of the causes of suffering." Visualize the person
attaining a state of freedom, peace, and joy.

Compassion for a neutral person
Bring to mind a person you are more distant from, and for whom you
have neutral feelings, such as a neighbor or someone at work. Visualize this
person in front of you, or think of her wherever she may be right now.
Spend some time contemplating the physical and mental pain that she is
probably experiencing at this time. Contemplate that she, just like you and
your loved ones, does not want to experience suffering, and wants to be
free of it, and feel that she deserves to be free. Then generate the wish for
her to be free. If you wish, you can use the phrases mentioned above, or
whatever other words you find helpful to generate a feeling of compassion. Imagine that the person's suffering disappears, and she becomes
peaceful, happy, and full of positive energy.

Compassion for an enemy or a difficult person
Bring to mind someone you dislike, whose behavior causes problems for
you and for others. Visualize this person sitting in front of you, or think
of him where he is right now. Contemplate that this person is a being
who wants to be free of suffering, just as you do. In fact, it's probably this
wish that motivates him to behave the way he does—he's just trying to
be happy and avoid problems.

   Go into his mind, and try to understand how he thinks, and why he
behaves this way. How do things appear from his perspective? Are there
disturbing, negative thoughts dominating his mind, causing him to see
things in certain ways, and to act the way he does? Try to understand the

causes and conditions that influenced him to be like this. Consider the possibility that there could be troubling circumstances in his life, either now or in the past, that influence him to be the way he is. Perhaps the difficult behavior we observe is a survival mechanism he developed in order to deal with these problems.

But it is also possible that there are no external problems causing him to be this way. His attitudes and behavior could be due to internal factors: the karmic imprints and habitual tendencies he created in his past lives and brought with him into this life. Either way, he is not in control of his mind and his actions. He is under the control of delusions, negative mental states.

Understand that he is suffering. Recall times when your own mind was dominated by one or more of the delusions—when you were full of rage, selfishness, or greed. Remember how disturbing and painful those experiences were, and how helpless you were in the face of these powerful emotions. That is what your enemy is going through right now. His mind is anything but peaceful and happy; it is in hell, tortured by delusions.

Mentally separate the person from his karma and delusions; understand that these are transitory factors in his mind, and not who he really is. His mind is basically pure, like the sky, and endowed with positive qualities: love, compassion, wisdom, and so on. These qualities are temporarily overshadowed by delusions, but they exist, and they can be developed and perfected. One day this person will be an enlightened being, free of all that is negative and complete in all that is positive.

Generate compassion for your enemy. Wish him to be free of the suffering that he is going through now, and the suffering he will probably experience in the future. Wish him to also be free of the causes of suffering: disturbing, negative mental states, and unskillful actions motivated by these. Think, "May you be free of all physical suffering. May you be free of all mental suffering. May you be free of the causes of suffering." As before, you can imagine this person's suffering, karma, and delusions vanishing, and he attains a state of peace, joy, and goodness.

Compassion for all beings

After meditating on one or more of the sections above, contemplate that all living beings are exactly the same in wanting to be free of suffering. No one likes pain or problems; everyone feels distress when unwanted experiences occur. Think of some of the problems human beings are experiencing right now in the world: war, hunger, poverty, homelessness, joblessness, anxiety, stress, loneliness, and so on. You can also think of the suffering of other beings such as animals: hunger and thirst, heat and cold, fear, being killed by other animals or by people, and so on. Generate compassion for all these beings by thinking, "They are no different from me; just as I wish to not suffer, so do they. May they be free of all their physical suffering. May they be free of all their mental suffering. May they be free of the causes of suffering." Visualize that all their suffering and causes of suffering disappear, and they become endowed with happiness, peace, and positive qualities.

DEDICATION

When you wish to end the meditation, dedicate the positive energy, or merit, you created to the attainment of liberation—freedom from all suffering and its causes—and enlightenment, for yourself and all other beings.

Meditation on Chenrezig

Chenrezig is a buddha who embodies the immeasurable, universal compassion of all enlightened beings. We too have the potential to develop boundless compassion, and contemplating Chenrezig can awaken this potential.

It is also beneficial to recite Chenrezig's mantra: *om mani padme hum* (pronounced *om mah-nee ped-may hoom*). A mantra is a series of syllables, usually in Sanskrit, that originate from an enlightened mind, and that help to purify and transform our own mind. Chenrezig's mantra expresses the pure energy of compassion that exists in every being. *Om* symbolizes the enlightened state we wish to attain. *Mani* means jewel, and symbolizes the "method" side of the path: compassion, love, and bodhichitta. *Padme* means lotus, and represents the wisdom side of the path, which blooms beautifully and fully out of the mud of samsara. *Hum* indicates inseparability; it refers to the inseparable union of method and wisdom on the path to enlightenment. Thus *om mani padme hum* means that by practicing compassion and wisdom inseparably, we can transform ourselves into enlightened beings and be of benefit to everyone.

If you are more comfortable visualizing another figure or symbol that represents compassion to you, feel free to do so. The point of the meditation is to get in touch with our innate energy of compassion and develop it further, so that we can feel it for more beings and be of greater benefit to the world.

Chenrezig

PREPARATION

Make yourself comfortable in a good position for meditation. Relax your body and mind. Let your awareness settle in the present moment by mindfully watching your breath for a few minutes.

MOTIVATION

Generate a positive motivation for doing the meditation. If possible, think that you are doing it in order to become enlightened for the benefit of all beings. Alternatively, think that you are doing it to make your life meaningful and beneficial for others.

MAIN MEDITATION

If you wish, while doing the meditation, you can imagine other people and beings sitting around you. Your mother is on your left, your father on your right; sisters and female relatives are next to your mother; brothers and male relatives are next to your father. Your friends are sitting behind you, and those you dislike are sitting in front of you. People for whom you have neutral feelings are around you, in all directions. Imagine as many people and beings as you can, comfortably.

Then, visualize in the space in front of you, at the level of your fore-head, Chenrezig, the Buddha who embodies pure, universal compassion. Every aspect of the visualization is made of light: transparent and radiant, like a rainbow. Chenrezig's body is of white light, dazzling like freshly fallen snow. His face is peaceful and smiling, gazing at you and at all the beings surrounding you with an expression of perfect love and compassion. He has four arms. His first two hands are together in front of his heart, holding a wish-fulfilling jewel; his second two are raised at the level of his shoulders, the right holding a crystal rosary and the left a white lotus. He is sitting in the full-lotus posture on a white moon disc that rests upon an open lotus. He wears exquisite silks and precious ornaments.

Be content with whatever you are able to visualize, and don't worry if the image does not appear clearly with all the details. The most important thing is to feel that Chenrezig (or whatever image you wish to use) is actually there in front of you, that you are in the presence of a manifestation of pure, universal loving-kindness and compassion.

Spend some time contemplating Chenrezig's compassion; try to get a feeling of it. His mind is fully aware, in every moment, of every painful experience, physical and psychological, of every being without exception. He has no anger or aversion, not even for a moment, but feels only pure compassion: wishing all of us to be free of all suffering and its causes. He sees clearly that our suffering is caused by ignorance and other delusions, as well as the actions we do under their influence. He understands that we are helplessly trapped in this painful situation, and thus he forgives us for all our faults and mistakes.

Look into your mind and check if there are any aspects of yourself that you are unable to accept and forgive. There may be unskillful, harmful actions you did in the past, or habitual tendencies you are unable to give up, or negative thoughts you are ashamed of and try to keep hidden. Reflect that Chenrezig sees all of these—in fact, he knows you better than you know yourself—but does not feel even the slightest aversion for you. He completely accepts you just as you are, loves you unconditionally, and is compassionately dedicated to helping you for all of time until you are free and enlightened. This is because he sees your pure buddha nature, and thus he knows that your negative qualities are transitory and not who you really are. Try to really feel Chenrezig's forgiveness and compassion for you.

Turn your mind to the people sitting around you—in particular those in front of you, the people you dislike—and contemplate that Chenrezig feels exactly the same way toward them. He accepts them just as they are, in spite of their imperfections and mistakes, and is compassionately dedicated to helping each and every one of them, until they are all enlightened. He sees them all as completely worthy of his love and compassion.

Now generate the wish to have in your own heart the same feeling of compassion that Chenrezig has: forgiveness, acceptance, love, and compassion for all beings without exception. You may want to make a prayer of request to Chenrezig, in your own words, asking him to help you achieve this. Then visualize streams of pure white light flowing from Chenrezig into you, filling every cell and atom of your body. The essence of this light is his immeasurable loving-kindness and compassion. It purifies all the negative aspects of your body and mind: sickness and other physical problems, all your past harmful thoughts and actions, and your habitual negative tendencies, especially those that are obstacles to immeasurable compassion. The light completely fills you with love, compassion, wisdom, and all other positive qualities. Your body feels light and blissful, your mind peaceful and clear.

The light from Chenrezig also radiates out to all the people and beings sitting around you, purifying their negative energy and filling them with bliss. Their minds are filled with positive energy, especially compassion and loving-kindness.

While visualizing this, you can recite the mantra, *om mani padme hum*, aloud or silently to yourself, as many times as you like. When you have finished the recitation, visualize that Chenrezig melts into white light, which dissolves into you. Imagine that your mind merges indistinguishably with Chenrezig's mind in an experience of complete purity, tranquillity, and bliss. Let your mind rest in this experience for a while. If ordinary thoughts or your usual sense of I start to arise, think that they are not who you really are. Let go of these thoughts, and return your attention to the feeling of being inseparable from the qualities of Chenrezig's enlightened mind.

DEDICATION

When you are ready to conclude the meditation, dedicate the positive energy you have created that all beings, yourself and others, will attain Chenrezig's pure qualities—universal love, compassion, wisdom, and so on—and will become fully enlightened as quickly as possible.

O

Immeasurable Joy

May all beings never be separated from the happiness that is free from suffering.

Once, while traveling from India to Nepal, I had to stay overnight in Varanasi, a city in northern India famous for its temples and religious festivals. I arrived at my hotel about 9:00 p.m. to find the air filled with blaring Indian pop music—there was a wedding party going in the courtyard of the hotel. My heart sank. I thought I would not get any sleep that night. The hotel clerk assured me the party would be over by 11:00 p.m., but I was skeptical as I went to my room. The music was so loud it was difficult to concentrate on anything. Then I remembered a story I heard about my teacher, Lama Zopa Rinpoche, who was once in a similar situation. There was an all-night wedding party in the hotel across the street from the monastery where he was staying, but the music didn't bother him at all. Instead, he rejoiced in the happiness of the people at the party.

I decided to try that. I sat down and thought of what a joyous occasion it was for the couple, their family, and friends. I shared in their joy and wished them to have happiness, as well as love and compassion for each other, for the rest of their lives. I found that by filling my mind with such thoughts, I no longer minded the music. Rejoicing in their joy transformed my mind.

Taking delight in the happiness, success, and good fortune of others is one of the ways that we practice the third immeasurable thought, immeasurable joy. In fact, you will find it's not that hard to find joy in the happiness of others. It is something we already experience, naturally. When we see children playing joyfully, we feel happy too. We feel happy when a loved one wins a prize, passes an exam, makes a new friend, finds an exciting new job, or brings a child into the world. The practice of immeasurable joy cultivates this state of mind further, beyond our circle of friends and family. We can learn to share in the joy of all beings. It's actually an easy way to feel happy.

Immeasurable joy is often called "sympathetic joy," because it is not a private joy, such as we might feel from winning a tennis game. Rather it is a joy that is outer-directed and inclusive of others. Immeasurable joy is like a further extension of immeasurable loving-kindness, because it wishes everyone to experience happiness not only now, but far into the future. One way of developing the third immeasurable thought, as expressed in the prayer, is wishing all beings to have happiness that is free from suffering. This means wishing them to have fortunate rebirths and good experiences in all of their future lives, as long as they are in samsara, the cycle of death and rebirth. However, since samsaric happiness is temporary and unreliable, we also wish beings to attain the sublime peace and happiness of liberation, and thus be free forever from samsara and all its problems. In order to attain this state, they must follow the path to liberation which consists of ethics, concentration, and wisdom. Therefore, we wish all beings to learn, understand, and practice this path.

Immeasurable joy can be cultivated in the same way as loving-kindness. You first generate it for individuals, starting with a friend, then gradually move on to a neutral person, an enemy, yourself, and all beings. You can use phrases such as, "May you always have good rebirths and pleasant, positive experiences in all your future lives. And may you quickly attain liberation, freedom from all suffering."

We often find it difficult, though, to even share in other people's ordinary joy or success, no less wishing them the joy that comes from freedom from suffering. We can begrudge people their simple joys if they encroach on our turf. We can also feel jealous of others' good fortune. If a colleague at work is promoted to a position we had hoped to get ourselves, we may put on a smile and say, "How wonderful; I am so happy for you," but in our heart there is nothing but pain: "Why him and not me? I wanted that position so badly. It's not fair."

If we meet a person who has more knowledge, abilities, or talent than we do, our heart may become tight and closed, unable to feel admiration or joy. What has happened is that our ego and self-centeredness have reared their heads, blocking loving-kindness and joy, and making us miserable. One of my teachers, Ribur Rinpoche, once explained that because of self-centeredness we tend to compare ourselves with others and end up with three kinds of feelings. Toward those who seem to be better than us (in terms of intelligence, attractiveness, social standing, wealth, and so forth) we feel jealousy, or envy. Toward those we consider inferior to us, we feel proud, arrogant, and condescending. Toward those who seem to be roughly equal to us, we feel competitive, always wanting to get one step ahead of them by showing that we know something they don't, or that we can do something they can't. This is such a sad situation. Although we long for happiness, we create so much unhappiness by getting caught up in this tangle of comparisons! The Chinese have a saying: If you compare yourself with others, you will die of frustration.

Overcoming Jealousy

Feeling jealous toward those who seem to be better or have more is the main obstacle to immeasurable joy. It is a particularly ugly, painful state of mind, because it is a concoction of two mental toxins—attachment and hatred. We have attachment to something another person has or has attained, and hate the fact that he has it instead of us. It's impossible to be happy when we have jealousy; it makes us tense and closed-off. While others are celebrating joyfully, our heart is burning with envy and resentment. It can lead us to behave in childish or nasty ways that win criticism rather than the respect we seek.

Let's look more carefully at the mechanism behind jealousy. Its root is self-grasping ignorance, which we started discussing in chapter 2—the belief in a solid, permanent self or I that exists all on its own, without depending on anything else. Ignorance then gives rise to self-cherishing, attachment, and hatred. Self-cherishing feels, "My happiness is my number one priority, and I need x, y, and z in order to be happy. I have x and y but not z, so I'm not happy. I notice that Sally over there has z, and I can't stand it!" It sounds primitive, and it is, but that's what we do.

Jealousy may also be connected with pride. It is pride that wants to be the best, and can't bear it if someone is better than us. However, beneath pride is usually a lack of confidence, a sense of inner impoverishment: "If I'm not the best, then I'm worthless." All these attitudes are unhealthy and unrealistic—they don't see things in a correct way—and lead only to misery, not happiness.

Don't despair! As we have seen, there are methods we can use to overcome negative mental states and to cultivate loving-kindness. Familiarity with these methods should decrease the possibility of jealousy arising in the first place. It takes time to transform our mind, though, so we will probably still sometimes find ourselves feeling envious. What can we do in such cases? Actually, the best antidote to jealousy is joy, sharing in the other person's happiness instead of begrudging it. But if we're already caught up in envy, we may not be able to immediately switch our mind to feeling joyful. We need to first let go of the jealousy.

One way we can do that is to contemplate what is known in Buddhism as "dependent arising"—the fact that whatever exists and whatever happens depends on other factors, such as causes and conditions. We can think, "If Anthony got the promotion instead of me, perhaps he is more qualified, more capable of doing the job. This could be because of training and experience that he gained in this life, or it could be that he has more natural ability, which is due to karma from previous lives. At any rate, this happened because of factors for which he created the causes, and I did not create." This enables us to be more peaceful and accepting of the situation, and rejoice in Anthony's good fortune rather than feeling jealous. But it does not mean that we must always just accept things passively. If we think that our boss acted unfairly or that we really are more qualified for the job, we can certainly try to appeal our case. But that is a different matter from the jealous feelings that torment our mind.

Being jealous won't change anything, but rejoicing will (we'll talk about rejoicing more below). Jealousy is a negative state of mind resulting in negative experiences, whereas joy is a positive attitude that brings about the good experiences we wish for. If we can generate joy and admiration regarding others' good qualities, happiness, success, and so on, we are creating the causes to have similar experiences in the future.

It could also be helpful to do a reality check. We sometimes envy a person whose life seems perfect and problem-free, but thinking more carefully, we will realize that this is an illusion. This person is subject to many of the same problems we and all other humans have to go through, like sickness, aging, and death, and may even have some problems we don't have. Also, the impermanent nature of things means that the happiness or success she is enjoying is only temporary. Reflecting on these thoughts can help us let go of jealousy. However, we have to be careful that we don't end up gloating: "She thinks she's happy, but just wait and see. It's not real happiness and it won't last long." Even if her happiness is transitory, we can still feel joyful for her, and wish that her good fortune will last as long as possible. Isn't that a more positive, satisfying way to feel?

As dissatisfaction is one aspect of jealousy, an effective remedy is learning to be content with what we have and the way we are. In reality, we have so much to be thankful for and happy about, but we tend to ignore what's in our own life and poke our noses into other people's lives and then feel deprived. A good solution is to "count our blessings"—think about what we have and feel thankful: "Others may have more than me, but that's okay. What I have is good enough." It can also be helpful to think of those who are much less fortunate than ourselves, as we have discussed. It's usually not a good idea to compare ourselves with others, but it's okay to do it occasionally to counteract an unhealthy attitude such as depression, low self-esteem, or jealousy. It can restore our mind to a more balanced state, and clear the way to feeling joyful.

We can also consider that even if we did obtain those desired things that others have, we might still not be satisfied. If we have the habit of being dissatisfied with what we have and envious of others, getting what one person has might make us happy momentarily, but it's only a matter of time before we will see something that another person has and we don't, and again we will feel jealous. It's a never-ending cycle of suffering. Contentment, on the other hand, is a real blessing, a source of peace and happiness.

Rejoice!

In the Tibetan tradition, there is a practice known as "rejoicing." It is directly related to immeasurable joy (and in fact the English word *rejoicing* is from the same root as *joy* and derives from the idea of *filling with joy* or gladdening). The practice of rejoicing involves feeling happy about our own and others' positive qualities and actions, as we have been discussing. For example, when we recognize good qualities in others such as compassion, kindness, wisdom, calmness, or strength, or when we see or hear of someone doing a positive, beneficial action such as giving, we rejoice: "How wonderful that is. I am so happy about that." And we really mean it. The reasoning behind this feeling is that positive qualities and actions are the cause of happiness. When people engage in these, they bring benefit to themselves and others, now and in the future. This is exactly what we aspire for when we generate loving-kindness, so it's only right to be joyful when people are doing what we wish them to do.

However, rejoicing can also be obstructed by jealousy. Let's say we have a friend who is good-hearted and generous. We find out that she plans to donate $100 to a charity and we think, "Why does she have to give so much? It makes me look stingy. I only gave $5." Or perhaps we are interested in meditating, but have trouble sitting still for more than ten minutes. We notice someone who can sit without moving for an hour, looking utterly peaceful, and we find it unbearable. Out of jealousy, we may even try to convince our generous friend not to make such a large donation, or do something to disturb the meditator's peace. Feeling jealous of and interfering with others' positive actions only makes matters worse; we create unskillful karma, and remove ourselves further from being generous ourselves, or being able to meditate well. It makes much more sense to rejoice, because appreciating others' positive qualities and deeds encourages us to be like them. If we can think, "How wonderful if I could do the same myself," we mentally steer ourselves in that direction.

We also need to rejoice in our own positive actions and qualities. This is a very effective antidote to self-hatred and depression. Depression is sometimes aptly described as *anger directed at oneself.* It usually focuses on what's wrong with us—our past mistakes, our habitual negative attitudes and tendencies, our weaknesses and shortcomings—exaggerates them, and ignores our positive traits and deeds. It constructs and believes in a negative self-image: that I am absolutely hopeless, unlovable, and unworthy.

Rejoicing in our own goodness counteracts this tendency. We bring to mind positive qualities we have and beneficial things we have done— acts of kindness, generosity, and service; efforts to improve ourselves; studying and practicing spiritual teachings; trying to live ethically, and so on—feel joyful about these, and wish to continue doing them in the future. There is nothing wrong with feeling good about our positive actions, as long as it doesn't turn into pride. Pride is a puffing up of our ego. We feel that we are better than others and look down on them. (More information about pride and how to remedy it will come in section two, verse 2.) Rejoicing is simply feeling happy about good things we've done or good qualities we have, without feeling we are superior to anyone else. In fact, *everyone* has good qualities and does good actions, and everyone has the same potential to transform themselves and become enlightened. So ultimately no one is better than anyone else!

Rejoicing itself is a positive action that creates positive energy, or "merit." Merit is like fuel that enables us to progress along the spiritual path and reach liberation and enlightenment; it is also the cause of happiness and good experiences along the way. Rejoicing is relatively easy to practice—we can even do it lying in bed or at the beach—and it immediately makes our mind more positive, happy, and peaceful. All we have to do is think of and feel happy about positive things people are doing, like helping the needy, making donations, living ethically, practicing meditation, or even just being kind and caring to their family, friends, and neighbors.

But we must be careful to avoid *negative* rejoicing: feeling happy about actions that are deluded, harmful, or unskillful. For example, it would not be appropriate to rejoice when our country, involved in a war with another country, shoots missiles at the enemy and kills many people, or when a friend gleefully tells us how he cheated someone in a business deal and made a huge profit. This kind of rejoicing is unwise and results in suffering. We ourselves create negative karma, and we are supporting the negative actions of others.

Initially, practicing joy or rejoicing may seem forced or artificial. But even if we don't *really* feel happy about someone's good fortune, success, or positive actions, it's helpful to say or think the words, "I'm so happy. I rejoice." Doing this will probably bring some instant benefit: our mind will feel lighter and brighter. And since we want to be happy, once we realize that rejoicing feels so much better than being jealous, depressed, and judgmental, our mind will naturally gravitate to it, and we will find it increasingly easy to do. As they say in the Twelve-Step Traditions, "Fake it 'til you make it."

A Meditation on Rejoicing

This is a meditation in which we can practice rejoicing in the positive qualities and actions of ourselves and others. What I have written are just suggestions; feel free to bring to mind other examples of people and their qualities and actions that bring benefit to others, as well as to themselves.

There are several parts to the meditation, starting with oneself, then going on to others. You can do as many parts as you like in each session, and spend as much time as you wish on each part. It's also good to bring this practice into your daily life, by rejoicing when you see or hear of positive, beneficial things people are doing.

PREPARATION

Sit comfortably in a good position for meditation. Relax your body and mind. Let your awareness settle in the present moment by mindfully watching your breath for a few minutes.

MOTIVATION

Generate a positive, altruistic motivation for doing the meditation. For example, you can think that you are doing it to increase the positive energy in your mind, in order to have more joy to share with others, and to make your life as meaningful and beneficial as possible. You can also think that you are doing it in order to become enlightened so that you can bring the greatest benefit to all beings.

REJOICING IN YOUR OWN GOODNESS

Think back over your life, or over the past few weeks or months, and bring to mind things you have done that were positive—beneficial to others, to yourself, or to both. With each of these actions you recall, feel a sense of rejoicing: "That was a good thing. I'm glad I did it, and would like to do it again." You might recall acts of giving money or other material things; giving love, for example, spending time with someone who was lonely or depressed; giving protection, helping beings who were frightened or in danger; giving spiritual advice, helping others learn how to transform themselves in positive ways. Perhaps you have been trying to live ethically, refraining from harmful, unwise actions such as killing, stealing, lying, or speaking hurtful words, and to act in ways opposite to those.

Have you worked on being more patient, kind, compassionate? Have you made attempts to practice meditation, to make your mind more subdued and positive, less out-of-control and negative? Think of other positive actions. Rejoice in all of these, and feel the wish to continue doing them in the future.

REJOICING IN OTHERS' GOODNESS

Here, you could start thinking of those you know who have done beneficial acts, then move on to others you have heard of in the world at large who have acted beneficially. Think of as many positive actions as you can, and rejoice: feel happy that people are doing these, benefiting others as well as themselves, and wish that they continue doing them as much as possible. You can think of extraordinary acts of kindness and generosity done by some people—donating organs to save another's life, risking their lives to rescue those in danger, working to help people suffering in very difficult circumstances such as war, natural disasters, or famine, or making large donations to enable such work to be carried out. You can also think of the ordinary acts of kindness people do on a daily basis: parents taking care of their children; children caring for their aged parents; teachers educating their students; doctors and nurses treating their patients; veterinarians caring for animals; police protecting citizens from crime; firemen and ambulance drivers rushing to help people in emergency situations; farmers, factory workers, and shopkeepers working to provide us with food, clothing, and other necessities, and so on. You can also rejoice in simple acts of benevolence such as people smiling, being friendly to each other, and treating each other with kindness and consideration.

REJOICING IN THE GOODNESS OF RELIGIOUS PRACTITIONERS

Now rejoice in the qualities and actions of people who devote their lives to religious study and practice: living ethically and non-harmfully; spending hours each day in prayer and meditation; working on purifying and transforming their minds; helping people in need such as the elderly, the sick, the dying, prisoners, addicts, orphans, those suffering from mental illness, and so on. Contemplate how beneficial these activities are for others, for the world, and for themselves. Rejoice and generate the wish that these activities will continue as much as possible.

REJOICING IN THE GOODNESS OF SPIRITUAL TEACHERS

These are people who devote their lives to learning and practicing spiritual paths, and then teaching others so that they too can follow such paths. We need spiritual teachers who can teach and guide us, and who serve as examples or role models, showing us what we can be. Contemplate the great service such people provide to us, to the world. Rejoice in what they are doing and wish it to continue without end.

REJOICING IN THE GOODNESS OF BUDDHAS AND BODHISATTVAS

Buddhas are beings who attained enlightenment after many lifetimes of practicing the path. Therefore, over countless lives, they practiced giving, ethics, patience, joyous effort, concentration, and wisdom—motivated by compassion and love for all beings without exception. Their sole wish was to attain enlightenment, the fulfillment of the highest potential of the mind, so they could help all beings be free of suffering and attain enlightenment. And after attaining enlightenment they have continued to work with love and compassion for all beings, every moment, every day, without break.

Bodhisattvas are those who are still following the path to enlightenment, practicing the six perfections with the goal of becoming buddhas to benefit all beings. So they, too, are completely and continuously dedicated to the welfare of all beings throughout space.

The principal way that buddhas and bodhisattvas help is by teaching us how to stop creating the causes of suffering, and how to create the causes of happiness, especially the ultimate happiness of liberation and enlightenment. Contemplate the extraordinary qualities and beneficial deeds of these beings, rejoice, and wish that they will continue to do this work forever.

DEDICATION

Conclude the meditation by dedicating the positive energy you created that everyone, yourself and others, will continue to engage in goodness as much as possible, and that all beings may quickly attain liberation and enlightenment.

7
Immeasurable Equanimity

*May all beings abide in equanimity, free from attachment and anger
that hold some close and others distant.*

It is possible that when we meditate on loving-kindness, compassion, and joy, we may say or think, "May all beings have happiness. May all beings be free from suffering. May all beings be joyous," but what our heart actually feels is: "May all beings be happy, free from suffering, and joyful—*except* for that person, and that person, and that person." Our thoughts become partial, not immeasurable.

This can occur because our usual way of relating to others is the exact opposite to the fourth of the immeasurable thoughts: equanimity. Without equanimity, the other three thoughts—love, compassion, and joy—will not be immeasurable. They will contain caveats, biases, provisos, and exceptions. Equanimity is an unbiased, impartial attitude that regards all beings as equally deserving of our respect and concern, our love and compassion. The prayer above expresses the wish for all beings to have equanimity, but realistically we must start by developing it in our own mind.

As we have seen in the meditations, we tend to divide beings into three groups, and have three very different attitudes toward them. There are those we regard as "friends"—we like them, feel happy when we see them, and want to be close to them. We shower them with love, affection, and gifts. However, our love is usually not completely pure, but is mixed with selfish attachment and possessiveness.

The second group includes those we dislike, our so-called "ene-mies"—we feel unhappy when we see or think of them, or even hear their name, and we want to stay far from them. If we see them walking down the street, we go out of our way to avoid meeting them. We have thoughts of hatred and animosity toward them, and treat them coldly or even spitefully.

Then there is a third group, "strangers," people toward whom we have neutral feelings. We neither like nor dislike them, but feel a kind of uncar-ing indifference. We do not hate them, but we just don't think of extend-ing our loving-kindness and compassion to them. Most of the people and beings in the world belong to this group. For example, when we walk through a busy airport or train station, or go shopping in a crowded mall, although there may be hundreds of people around us, we feel nothing for them, as if they were mindless mannequins.

What's wrong with this situation? For one thing, we are not fulfilling our potential as human beings. We have the ability to feel love and com-passion for all beings, but we reserve these feelings for a select few. And the basis for deciding who these lucky ones are is our attitude of self-centeredness. Let's take a look at how it works. As you know by now—and as the teachings of Buddhism will continue to remind you at every opportunity—the very root of all our problems is ignorance, in particu-lar self-grasping ignorance, which believes in a real, permanent, inde-pendently existing self or I. Of course, this I is just a fabrication of the mind. It doesn't really exist, but ignorance doesn't realize this and unques-tioningly believes in its existence, like the citizens of Oz believing there is a gigantic, powerful wizard living in the palace in the Emerald City. Self-grasping ignorance gives rise to self-importance, the attitude that says I am at the center of the universe, my happiness is more important than any-one else's, and my needs and wishes are top priority.

Out of ignorance and self-centeredness, we also have lists of likes and dislikes with which we judge people, things, events, and experiences, always from the perspective of *I* or *me*. "I like that person because he makes me feel good, says nice things to me, and gives me presents, but I don't like that person because she makes me feel uncomfortable, doesn't say or do nice things to me, and is sometimes unkind to me. And that person over there doesn't make me feel good or bad, so I don't care about him at all. He's just a nobody." The attitudes involved here are attachment, hatred, and ignorance, respectively—the three poisons, the main causes of suffering, and the main factors that keep us in samsara. When we allow our mind to get caught up in these attitudes, we perpetuate our existence in samsara, rather than progressing in the direction of freedom and enlightenment.

You might find this explanation difficult to accept, or even understand. So it might be helpful look at the some of the more immediate problems caused by our biased, non-equal attitudes toward others. For one thing, they make us like Dr. Jekyll and Mr. Hyde—we are sweet and loving to one person, mean and nasty to another. Does that feel right? We've discussed the problems with these three poisons already, but it will be helpful to quickly revisit them in the context of equanimity, because equanimity is all about dissolving the distinctions that help to fuel these mental toxins and that were caused by them in the first place.

The Results of Attachment, Hatred, and Indifference

Attachment to loved ones may seem like a good thing, but it causes problems. We can become possessive of people and want to control and manipulate them. We have expectations of our friends, then become angry at them if they don't comply. It can lead to jealousy, when our loved one gives her attention to someone else; to fear, dreading the thought that something might happen to our relationship; to dependency, thinking we can't be happy without the other person; and to utter misery, if the relationship does come to an end. In fact, all the problems that occur in relationships can be traced to attachment.

The problems caused by hatred of others are easy to recognize. Hatred makes our mind disturbed and unhappy, and leads us to harm others and create negative karma, thus producing suffering for ourselves in the future.

Even when we feel our anger is justified, clinging to it is painful, like holding a hot coal in our hand. If we don't want pain, we should just let go of it.

Indifference toward strangers, neutral people, is also problematic. These people deserve our concern just as much as our friends do. Developing love and compassion for them is good for them, but it's also good for ourselves—we will have more happiness now, and we move closer to enlightenment. On the other hand, to withhold love and compassion from strangers is to restrict ourselves: we limit our happiness here and now, and we prevent ourselves from attaining liberation and enlightenment.

What can we do to remedy this situation and develop equanimity? One way is to gradually overcome the three attitudes that run counter to it. The most powerful antidote to possessive-attachment to loved ones is to meditate on impermanence. Everything changes, nothing lasts. One day death will separate us from the people we love. Separation could occur even before that if one of us gets a job overseas or if we quarrel and come to hate each other. The more attached we are, the more pain and stress we will suffer at this separation; therefore, it's wise to let go of attachment. But that doesn't mean giving up love! We can love people without being attached to them, by living with awareness and acceptance of the inevitable separation. We can appreciate and care for them now and at the same time be ready to say goodbye when the time comes.

To overcome anger toward enemies, we can reflect on the possible causes and conditions of the harm they give us: "Have I done anything to provoke him? Could it be some flaw in my personality he doesn't like? Perhaps I harmed him in a previous life and he's simply repaying me?" Recognizing that the problem may be due in part to something we ourselves did, knowingly or unknowingly, can help our mind be more accepting and tolerant, and less angry. Even if that is not the case, we can consider that the person's mind is under the control of delusions, and he can't help but act this way. There have been times when our own mind was in such a state, so we can remember what it's like, how painful it is. We can thus understand that the person must be suffering a lot now, and will suffer even more in the future, when his negative karma ripens. If we make our mind familiar with such thoughts, we can generate compassion and patient acceptance toward enemies.

To overcome uncaring indifference toward neutral persons, we can contemplate that they, just like ourselves and our loved ones, want to be happy and free of suffering, and deserve to be. We can also reflect on their kindness: "Without all those people, I would have no food, clothes, shelter, or public services. Without others, I could not develop ethics, generosity, patience, and the other positive qualities necessary for spiritual growth. Without others, life would be empty and meaningless." Furthermore, a stranger may not always be a stranger. When she helps us out in a difficult situation, or treats us with kindness, she can become a lifelong friend.

Mingling Friends, Enemies, and Strangers

There is also a meditation for developing equanimity in the *Lam Rim* (Path to Enlightenment) tradition of Tibetan Buddhism. It is actually the first step in developing bodhichitta, the aspiration to become enlightened for the benefit of all beings. The idea is that we need to cultivate equanimity initially to ensure that our cultivation of love, compassion, and bodhichitta really do include all beings without exception. At the end of the chapter, there are formal instructions for this practice, but I first want to introduce it here to discuss the thinking behind it. It will help us to understand what equanimity really means.

You begin the meditation by bringing to mind three people: a friend, a neutral person, and an enemy. Visualizing these three in front of you, you look at them one by one and examine your reasons for feeling the way you do toward each one. It's helpful to take an objective look at these reasons: are they good, solid reasons for liking, disliking, or feeling indifferent toward another person?

Following that, there are different points to contemplate. One of these is our old friend *impermanence*. We tend to feel that these relationships are permanent: the friend will be a friend forever; the enemy is someone we will never get along with; the neutral person will always be distant from us. Is this a realistic way of thinking? Think back over your life. Can you recall a person who was once a dear friend but later became an enemy, after a conflict or disagreement? And perhaps you can remember someone you hated at first, but later, after you got to know him better, became a friend? And the people who are now your friends and enemies were not always so; when you first met them, they were strangers, right? Thus relationships can and do change. Friends become enemies, enemies become friends, and strangers can become friends or enemies. In the meditation, it is helpful to imagine this happening, as a result of various causes and conditions that could occur.

I once did this meditation with a group of people, and in the discussion afterward a woman said that she put her husband in all three positions: friend, enemy, and stranger. I thought this was very insightful—it definitely happens that our feelings toward the same person can change, even in the course of one day, or one hour. And this illustrates another point about relationships: people are not friends, enemies, or strangers from their own side, in and of themselves. It is our mind that labels them so, depending on causes and conditions. Let's take this woman as an example, and imagine that her name is Anne and her husband's name is John. When Anne is in a good mood and John is behaving nicely, she has loving feelings for him, and he appears to her as a "friend." Later, she may be in a bad mood, and John is doing something she doesn't like, so he appears to her as an "enemy" and she is furious at him. On another occasion, Anne is completely involved in some work she has to finish by a certain deadline. She has no time or space in her mind to pay attention to John, so at that time he appears to her like a stranger, and she feels indifferent to him. Thus, "friend," "enemy," and "stranger" are labels our mind assigns to people, depending on the circumstances taking place at a given moment. A person is not a friend, enemy, or stranger independent of causes, conditions, and what our mind thinks about him.

We can also understand this by considering the ways in which one person appears to different people. John is a "friend" to his wife, Anne (most of the time, anyway!), and to his friends and family. But he is an "enemy" to someone he has a conflict with at work, and he is a "stranger" to people he passes in the street on his way to work. He is just one person, but viewed in three different ways by three different kinds of people. Contemplating this changeability can help to loosen our tight grasping to the idea of *real* friends, enemies, and strangers who seem to exist out there, independently, completely separate from us.

If you are open to the possibility of rebirth, you can also consider the idea that relationships can change from one life to another. It is said in the Buddhist teachings that we have been in every possible relationship with every being. Every being has been our mother, our father, our brother and sister, our spouse and partner, our child, our enemy, and so on. This means there is really no such thing as a stranger; no person with whom we have not been intimately connected many times in the past. Contemplating this can help diminish feelings of separateness and partiality, and enable us to feel greater equanimity.

It is also helpful to contemplate the ways in which we are all the same. Often we pay too much attention to the differences between ourselves and others, or between our friends and our enemies, and this leads to feeling disconnected and lonely. Differences do exist, of course—in terms of personality, ideas and beliefs, levels of intelligence, age, physical features, language, religion, and so on. However, these differences are mostly superficial, and depend on external factors that are transitory and subject to change. If we go deeper, to the core of our existence, we are all the same. We all want to be happy and to avoid suffering, problems, and bad experiences. Although each person's mind is unique and individual, all minds contain the same basic factors: positive states such as love, compassion, gratitude, wisdom; and negative states such as anger, attachment, jealousy, and self-centeredness. And, as we have discussed, the very nature of our minds is the same: clear and knowing, not permanently polluted by negative factors, and possessing the potential to be completely pure and positive. It is only because of the temporary negative mental states that we are confused and unhappy, and create problems for others and ourselves; we all have the same potential to free ourselves from this painful situation, and to become enlightened. Looking at others in the light of this understanding is a powerful method to balance our uneven feelings and help us develop greater impartiality.

Equal but Not Identical

Having equanimity does not mean that we will have the same relationship with everyone. This would be impossible. Even if we felt the wish to have a close friendship with each and every person, not everyone would feel that way toward us—there would be people who dislike us, or even hate us. Also, cultivating equanimity does not mean denying that there are some people who are kind to us, and others who are harmful. What it means is changing our attitudes, learning to stop differentiating between those we like and wish to help, those we dislike and do not want to help (and maybe even want to harm), and those we don't care about. Our mind/heart is open to everyone, equally.

A good analogy for the state of mind we're trying to develop is that of a doctor: he or she treats all patients equally, whether they are wealthy or poor, attractive or unattractive, a criminal or a law-abiding citizen, male or female, young or old, of the same religion or political party or a different one. Similarly, a person with equanimity has an open heart to all beings, seeing all beings as equally deserving of one's love, compassion, and concern.

An Equanimity Meditation

PREPARATION

Sit comfortably and spend a few minutes settling your mind in the present moment. Resolve to keep your mind focused on the meditation, and let go of any thoughts not related to the meditation.

MOTIVATION

Generate the intention to do this meditation for the benefit of all beings. Remember that equanimity is an essential basis for the cultivation of pure, unconditional love and compassion, and also for the ultimate attainment of enlightenment, to be able to work perfectly for the benefit of all beings.

MAIN MEDITATION

Think of a person you like, a "friend," and imagine this person sitting in front of you, a little to the left. Then think of a person you dislike, an "enemy," and imagine this person sitting in front of you, a little to the right. Finally, think of someone toward whom you have neutral feelings, a "stranger," and imagine this person sitting in front of you, between the other two. Do your best to keep the visualization of the friend, enemy, and stranger throughout the meditation.

First, focus on your *friend*, and ask yourself why you like this person. See if you can recognize that your reasons are mainly because of what she or he does for *you*.

Then look at the *person you dislike* and examine your reasons for feeling that way. Again, check if your ego is involved—for example, the person may have harmed you, or may behave in ways that you find unacceptable.

Then look at the *person you feel indifferent to*—why do you feel this way? Is your ego involved here as well—is it because this person has neither helped nor harmed you?

Take a step back and look at this situation objectively. How do you feel about having such different ways of relating to these three people? Do you think your reasons for doing so are good and solid ones?

Now ask yourself if you regard these relationships as permanent. Do you feel that you will always get along with your friend? …that you will never get along with your enemy? …that you will always be distant from the stranger? See if you can remember relationships you had in the past that changed: a friend becoming an enemy or a stranger, or vice versa.

Focus on your "friend" and imagine a situation in which this person does something hurtful or unacceptable. Would your feelings toward this person change? Recall that this person was not your friend before you became acquainted, and could cease to be your friend in the future.

Now turn your attention to your "enemy," and imagine this person doing something kind or helpful, such as praising you for something you did, or helping you fix your car which has broken down. Observe your feelings, and check to see if there is any change, any softening. Do you still feel that this person is a solid, permanent enemy?

Then look at the "stranger." This relationship could go either way, but since we are trying to develop more positive feelings for others, imagine the stranger doing something helpful, such as giving you the right directions when you are lost, or returning your wallet, which you dropped absent-mindedly. How would this affect your feelings toward this person?

Try to understand that relationships are not fixed and permanent. The person who is a friend today could become an enemy in the future, the enemy could become a friend, and the stranger could become either a friend or an enemy. It all depends on conditions and circumstances, and also on our mind. So it does not make sense to cling to these relationships as if they were carved in stone, existing forever.

If you accept the existence of past lives, consider the possibility that you have known these three people before, in other lifetimes. However, you were not always in the same kind of relationships with them. Your present friend may have been your enemy in another lifetime; try to imagine this.... Imagine that your enemy was someone very dear to you, a parent or sibling, or a close friend.... Imagine that the stranger was both a loved one, and an enemy, many times.... See how this affects your feelings toward these three people.

Another point to contemplate is that no one is a friend, enemy, or stranger independently, but they become so in dependence on how our mind labels them. The person you regard as a friend is seen by others as an enemy. The person you regard as an enemy is seen by some people as a beloved friend. And the person who is a stranger to you has friends who love him, and enemies who hate him.

We can also generate a more stable feeling of equanimity by reflecting on the ways in which *we are all the same*. Look at the three people in front of you and contemplate that the friend, enemy, and stranger all want happiness just as you do, and, just like you, they do not want to experience even the smallest problem. Also, all of you *deserve* to be happy and peaceful, and free of all suffering. Try to really feel this.

We are also equal in that we have the potential to free our minds from all negativities, develop our innate positive qualities, and achieve enlightenment, the highest state of peace and happiness. Everyone can—and *will*—become enlightened one day. We tend to focus on the superficial differences between ourselves and others, and feel separate and distant. If our thoughts and feelings were more in line with reality, we would see that everyone equally deserves our care and compassion.

Conclude the meditation by resolving to not cling so tightly to the relationships you presently have with others, as if they were permanent, and to recall the impermanent nature of people and relationships. Also resolve to pay less attention to the superficial differences between people, and to pay greater attention to the similarities.

DEDICATION

Remember the motivation you started with, and dedicate the positive energy and insight you created during the meditation to the well-being and happiness of all beings. May it be the cause for all of us to be happy, free of suffering, and enlightened.

Section
TWO

An Exploration of
The Eight Verses of Thought Transformation

In brief, the childish labor only for their own end,
While buddhas work solely for the welfare of others.
With a mind understanding the distinctions between
the failings of one and the advantages of the other,
We seek your blessings to enable us
To equalize and exchange ourselves for others.
—The Guru Puja[4]

As we have discussed, self-centerness is one of the main obstacles to developing loving-kindness and compassion. We often call it "the self-cherishing attitude," the one that causes us to silently chant to ourselves: "*me* first; my needs and wishes are more important than those of others." We all know what it feels like, and examples of it abound in our everyday experience. Perhaps there is an elderly woman living alone in your neighborhood. You are aware that she is lonely, has few visitors and has difficulty getting around or doing things for herself because of poor health. You may think about visiting her and offering your help, but you never get around to doing that because you think, "If I spend time talking with her or doing things for her, I'll have less time to do the things *I* want to do." We may not notice ourselves saying something like this to ourselves, because the me-first approach is very deep-seated. The practices we will explore in this chapter were developed to get to the heart of the me-first approach in any situation and turn it around, helping us gradually to overcome the self-cherishing that pervades our minds.

And, as we have seen, we *can* overcome selfishness and become more caring and compassionate. As the verse above says, we can "equalize and exchange ourselves for others": put others in the first position. It's a question of gradually training our mind, learning to transform our thoughts so that we are less concerned with *me*—what *I* want, what *I* need, what makes *me* happy—and more concerned about *others*. We come to think in terms of what *they* want and need, what makes *them* happy.

As we discussed in chapter 1, the tradition known as thought transformation, or *lojong* in Tibetan, provides some of the most immediate and direct methods to alter our me-first mentality on the spot. It was first transmitted in Tibet by Atisha Dipankara, an eleventh-century Indian master who was instrumental in the development of a pure tradition of Buddhism in Tibet. The teachings and practices of lojong are actively practiced today in all branches of Tibetan Buddhism, and as we noted earlier, are promoted by His Holiness the Dalai Lama and other lamas throughout the world.

To introduce you to the practice of thought transformation, I have chosen to use a succinct little text, *The Eight Verses of Thought Transformation*, written by a Tibetan meditator and teacher, Geshe Langri Tangpa, nearly one thousand years ago. Each of the eight four-line verses in his text highlights a different way in which we can transform our thoughts from being uncompassionate and self-centered, to being more compassionate and other-centered.

There are several ways to use the *Eight Verses* text. You can read it through from time to time, pausing to reflect on the meaning of each verse. Better yet, you can memorize it, so that the verses become part of your mind-stream. This way, when you find yourself in one of the situations described in the text, the appropriate verse might suddenly pop up in your mind, as if giving you advice on how to handle that situation.

There is also a way of using the *Eight Verses* as part of a daily meditation practice. You can think of or visualize the Buddha or Chenrezig in front of you, read or recite the verses, and pray for blessings and inspiration to be able to put the meaning of each verse into practice in your daily life.[5]

The practice of thought transformation, and of compassion itself, is truly challenging. Initially we may feel unable actually to practice the *Eight Verses*. Even so, merely reading through them can give us inspiration as to what can be achieved. Moreover, if we are willing to invest time and energy in the practice of training our mind, we will definitely experience a transformation.

The Eight Verses of Thought Transformation by Geshe Langri Tangpa

1

With the thought of attaining enlightenment
For the welfare of all beings,
Who are more precious than a wish-fulfilling jewel,
I will constantly practice holding them dear.

2

Whenever I am with others
I will practice seeing myself as the lowest of all,
And from the very depth of my heart
I will respectfully hold others as supreme.

3

In all actions I will examine my mind
And as soon as a disturbing emotion arises,
Endangering myself and others,
I will firmly confront and avert it.

4

Whenever I see beings of bad nature
And those oppressed by intense negativity and suffering,
I will practice holding such rare ones dear,
As if I had found a precious treasure.

5

When others, out of jealousy,
Mistreat me with abuse, insults, and the like,
I will practice accepting defeat
And offering the victory to them.

6

Even if someone I have benefited
And in whom I have placed great hopes
Hurts me very badly,
I will practice seeing that one as my sublime teacher.

7

In short, I will offer directly and indirectly
Every benefit and happiness to all beings, my mothers.
I will practice in secret taking upon myself
All their harmful actions and sufferings.

8

May all these practices be undefiled by the stains
Of the eight worldly concerns,
And by perceiving all phenomena as illusory,
May I be released from the bondage of attachment.

Verse 1: The Preciousness of All Living Beings

With the thought of attaining enlightenment
For the welfare of all beings,
Who are more precious than a wish-fulfilling jewel,
I will constantly practice holding them dear.

A wish-fulfilling jewel is a mythical gem that is said to grant whatever mundane wishes we may have, such as a nice car, money, a beautiful mansion, good health, and so on. This verse states that other beings are more precious than a wish-fulfilling jewel. The reason for this is that a wish-fulfilling jewel is unable to provide genuine, long-term happiness or peace of mind. As we saw in chapter 2, genuine happiness—which includes the ordinary happiness we experience in our everyday lives, as well as the sublime happiness of liberation and enlightenment—comes from positive states of mind and beneficial actions, and these are impossible without others. Let's see how this works.

The main source of whatever good things we have in this life—food, clothing, shelter, loving family and friends, a satisfying job, a healthy body, a happy mind, and so on—is the positive karma we created in past lifetimes. A large proportion of our good karma is created in relation to other beings; in fact, without others we would not be able to engage in meritorious practices such as giving, ethics, and patience. Therefore, one way that beings are precious is that they give us opportunities to create the causes of happiness in our present and future lives.

Another way that they are precious is by providing us with what we need to enjoy life. As discussed earlier, we are dependent on others for everything: our body comes from our parents, who also gave us the love and care we needed to grow, and who were our first teachers. Our friends fulfill our need for companionship and intimacy. Other people produce, package, and sell the food we eat each day. All the knowledge and skills we have were taught to us by others. Everything we own, use, and enjoy comes from others: our house, furniture, electricity, clothes, books, music, sports facilities, transportation—everything. Imagine what your life would be like without the existence of other people!

But the main reason other beings are precious is that without them we would not be able to attain enlightenment. Enlightenment, or Buddhahood, means never having to experience even a moment of suffering—you're free forever from all problems and suffering—and you experience continuously the greatest happiness and peace of mind. The purpose of attaining enlightenment, however, is not to just sit back and enjoy happiness and peace, it's so that you can help others to become free of their suffering and lead them to attain enlightenment as well. The motivation to attain enlightenment is the loving, compassionate wish to benefit others. But we cannot develop loving-kindness if there is nobody in need of love. Nor can we develop compassion without becoming aware of the suffering of others. Similarly, how could we practice generosity if there were no beings in need of food, money, medicine, protection, comfort, spiritual guidance, and so on? And with whom could we practice patience if we never met anyone who stirred up our anger?

We cannot attain any of the stages or realizations of the spiritual path without other beings. Thus they are very precious, far more precious than a Mercedes-Benz, a million dollars, or a wish-fulfilling jewel. When we realize how precious others are, we practice "holding them dear," which means we respect them, cherish them, care for them, avoid giving them any kind of harm, and do what we can to help them. Others are not a problem for us: they are the very seed of enlightenment.

Verse 2: Developing Humility and Respect

> *Whenever I am with others*
> *I will practice seeing myself as the lowest of all,*
> *And from the very depth of my heart*
> *I will respectfully hold others as supreme.*

In the first verse, we start to view other beings as precious and important.

Here, in the second verse, we go a step farther and learn to see them as more important than ourselves. Seeing ourselves as the lowest of all, as the text says, does not mean putting ourselves down or hating ourselves, as in thinking, "Oh, I'm hopeless. I'm worthless. I'm the worst person in the world." It means that we need to overcome pride. Pride is based on self-grasping ignorance—belief in a real, inherently existing I—and causes us to look down on others, and even mistreat them. We can be proud of our intelligence or knowledge, wealth or status, physical appearance or strength, or even our meditative abilities and experiences. However, pride is one of the biggest hindrances to true spiritual development. In order to grow spiritually, we need to be humble and respectful toward others—to cherish them and keep our mind open to learning from them—and pride is the very opposite of such an attitude. Pride can even make us feel superior to spiritual teachers and those who sincerely want to help us, and thus closes our mind to accepting their valuable advice and help.

We need to differentiate between pride and self-confidence: pride involves feeling superior to and looking down upon others, whereas a healthy sense of self-esteem or self-confidence involves recognizing and acknowledging our good qualities, achievements, abilities, and so forth, without going to the extent of feeling egotistical, arrogant, and thinking we are better than others. Self-confidence is actually an essential quality in spiritual practice; if we didn't believe in our ability to transform ourselves, become enlightened, and help others, we wouldn't even try.

As we discussed when we were exploring immeasurable joy and the act of rejoicing, pride makes us mentally compare ourselves to other people. When we find that we are in some way better, this fuels our feelings of self-importance: "I'm more intelligent than him, I'm more attractive than her, I'm better educated, I'm more talented." When we feel superior to others, we tend to be more critical and judgmental of them. Quietly, in our mind, we make lists of other people's faults and mistakes, and look down on them—as if we had no faults of our own!

On the other hand, if we find that the person we're comparing ourselves to is in some way superior, we feel jealous and resentful, because *we* want to be superior to *them. All* these attitudes are unhealthy. They disturb our mind and obstruct our spiritual development. They also prevent us from having positive and satisfying relationships with others. How can we really love and care about others, when we cannot even respect them?

There is a story from the life of Milarepa, an esteemed Tibetan Buddhist saint, that illustrates the disadvantages of pride. Three attractive young women, all dressed up in their finest clothes, came upon a poor, thin, bedraggled-looking man sleeping by the roadside. They were shocked by his appearance and one of them exclaimed: "Oh, I pray that I shall never become like *that!*" The man was Milarepa, and his poor appearance was the result of long years spent meditating in caves, living on little more than nettles. (His complexion even took on a green tinge.) He was actually a buddha—through his strong practice of meditation he had attained the state of enlightenment and his mind was completely pure—but he didn't look so great on the outside. Milarepa was not really asleep and when he heard the young woman's comment, he opened his eyes and said: "You couldn't be like me even if you wanted to!" When the young women realized who he was, they felt ashamed, begged his forgiveness, and requested him to teach them the Dharma, the Buddhist spiritual teachings.

One way to decrease pride and increase humility and respect for others is to train ourselves to see their good qualities rather than their faults. That is what this verse is all about. It's not telling us to put ourselves *down*, but rather to stop putting others down and ourselves *up*. Instead of focusing on our own qualities and on other peoples' faults and mistakes, we should be mindful of our limitations and focus on the good qualities of others. It's very easy to see faults in others and to criticize them, but once we realize that this does no good, we can train ourselves to do the opposite. We can always find something good in others, even in the worst person in the world. So try to always look for good qualities in others and to remember the positive things they've done.

Atisha, the one who brought thought transformation practice to Tibet, said, "Look for your own faults; don't look for those of others.

Hide your own good qualities; don't hide those of others." If we take this verse to heart and practice it, we will become more humble, more respectful toward others, and less critical. As a result, our mind will be happier, less negative, and our relationships with others will improve.

Another antidote to pride is contemplating that we are dependent on others for whatever it is we take pride in. Our body came from our parents, our knowledge and skills were learned from our teachers, our material possessions were produced by others, and so on. Perhaps the only thing we can truly call our own is our mind, but even there, the positive mental states we may feel proud of are dependent on others. Remembering impermanence is also helpful: due to the constantly changing nature of things, it's not certain that we will always have the things we are proud of. Wealth, health, beauty, fame, power, and even a clear, intelligent mind are transient, dependent on conditions we have no control over. Learning to think more realistically in these ways will deflate our false sense of arrogance and enable us to be more humble and respectful of others.

Verse 3: Cultivating Mindfulness

In all actions I will examine my mind
And as soon as a disturbing emotion arises,
Endangering myself and others,
I will firmly confront and avert it.

There are several ways of practicing mindfulness; one involves observing the mind and being on the lookout for disturbing emotions such as anger or aversion, attachment, jealousy, and pride. Such attitudes are harmful both to ourselves and to others. They harm ourselves by making our mind agitated and unpeaceful. They are harmful to others because they can impel us to speak harshly or act aggressively. In addition to hurting others, such actions will also bring us further problems and pain in the future. As we have discussed, all suffering is the result of previous negative actions committed under the influence of disturbing emotions.

Letting ourselves be controlled by negative emotions strengthens such habitual tendencies, and creates obstacles to our spiritual development. In future lives, we will have difficulty meeting spiritual teachings and teachers who can guide us on the path to liberation and enlightenment. Instead, we will find ourselves in detrimental circumstances and among people who nurture our negative qualities; thus we will fall deeper and deeper into confusion and suffering.

To protect ourselves and others from the harmful effects of disturbing emotions, we need to guard our mind with mindfulness, recognize such attitudes when they arise, and do something about them before they become strong enough to influence our behavior. There are several ways we can "confront and avert" our disturbing attitudes. One approach we have already seen in the earlier chapters is applying an antidote, something opposite to that particular disturbing emotion, such as meditating on compassion as an antidote to anger, or on joy as an antidote to jealousy. Another way is simply to let it go. Disturbing emotions, as we know, are not permanent, fixed aspects of our personality. They are temporary mental states that come and go in the mind. They arise when the right causes and conditions have come together, exist for a short time, and then disappear. If we take them too seriously, and identify with them, we give them undue strength and validity, and that makes it easier for them to take control of us. So, use the antidote we discussed in chapter 1: de-identify with thoughts and emotions. Instead of thinking: "I am angry," try thinking: "Anger is in my mind." Remind yourself that it is just an experience, a mental state that comes and goes in the mind, and see if you can just let it go. Let it go out of your mind, like a cloud drifting away, or like a bubble that bursts and disappears. Do not let it stay and disturb your mind.

Of course, there will be times when neither of these methods will work. For example, sometimes our anger is so strong that we just cannot let go of it or replace it with compassion or love. It takes hold of our mind and we can't forget it. In this case it is good to think about the many faults of anger we discussed earlier. Reminding ourselves of the drawbacks of anger and the other disturbing emotions can help us to generate the wish to avoid them and turn our mind to more positive attitudes.

At times, delusions arise very abruptly and we have no opportunity to work on them. We may get angry at work when we are criticized by our boss or a colleague, but have no chance to sit and meditate on the faults of anger, or on its antidotes of love and patience. In such a situation, we should try to keep the anger in our mind, keep it from spilling over into our speech or behavior—that is, try to avoid saying or doing anything out of anger, since that would just bring more problems. We may need to do something to keep calm, like taking a few deep breaths, counting to ten, saying a prayer or mantra, or leaving the room until we have cooled down.

But these are merely short-term ways of dealing with anger, to avoid losing control and doing something we would later regret. They enable us temporarily to restrain our anger, but not to get to its root and really deal with it. So what we need to do, when we have cooled down and have some time and space, is to sit down, think back over what happened, and try to understand why we got angry. With clear thinking, we may be able to recognize mistakes we made—for example, being too quick to take offense, having unreasonable expectations of the other person, not really understanding the other person's point of view, or just not having enough patience. Learning from our mistakes, we can think over how we might react differently if we were to find ourselves in a similar situation in the future. We might even be able to transform our attitude toward the person we got angry at, replacing our anger with more positive feelings such as acceptance or compassion.

Verse 4: Cherishing Those Who Are Difficult

Whenever I see beings of bad nature
And those oppressed by intense negativity and suffering,
I will practice holding such rare ones dear,
As if I had found a precious treasure.

This verse mentions several types of difficult people: those of "bad nature" (for example, a corrupt politician or CEO), and those who are "oppressed by intense negativity" (which could include cruel dictators, murderers, gangsters, and drug-dealers). How does your mind usually react to such people? Are you able to see them with eyes of compassion, or do you feel angry and judgmental, and even wish them to suffer? Our patience and compassion can also be challenged when we encounter "those oppressed by intense suffering," such as addicts, alcoholics, or those afflicted with severe physical or mental illnesses; we may feel uneasy and want to keep our distance rather than offering a helping hand. Although it is quite understandable to have such feelings, this verse is advising us to regard such people as especially dear, like a precious treasure.

Why? It is relatively easy to deal with people who are well-mannered, kind, and healthy—in their company we may even believe we have over-come our anger and achieved the perfection of patience. But when it comes to difficult people or those in complicated situations, our positive feelings are really put to the test. Such people give us the opportunity to recognize the limits of our patience and kindness, and the need to put more effort into cultivating these qualities.

Difficult people do not pose a problem for buddhas and bodhisattvas. Spiritually mature beings like these never feel fear or aversion toward anyone; they experience only love and compassion equally for all living beings. We too can learn how to keep our hearts open to even the most challenging people, by working on changing our attitudes and percep-tions. One way of doing this is to contemplate, "These people want to be happy and free from suffering, just as I do. The reason for their destruc-tive behavior (or disturbing appearance) is the presence of strong delusions and negative imprints in their minds. Their behavior and appearance are reflections of the delusions and imprints obscuring their minds. But delu-sions are temporary, not permanent. Like all beings, these people have the potential to attain enlightenment because their real nature is pure and positive. One day they will be buddhas, completely free from the delusions that are causing so many problems right now."

The thought transformation teachings advise us to separate a person from his or her delusions, and to attribute their unskillful behavior to the delusions rather than to the person. For example, if we hear of someone being convicted of murder or fraud, instead of blaming the person and feeling angry and judgmental, we should blame the delusions in his mind—ignorance, greed, hatred, or whatever—that motivated him to commit the crime. Then, it is easier to be tolerant and kind-hearted toward the person, and feel the compassionate wish for him to be free from his suffering and delusions.

It's also helpful to reflect that this person probably has *more* suffering than other people, and thus is in greater need of kindness and compassion. There is an account of a Tibetan lama who visited one of the former Nazi concentration camps in Germany that had been converted into a museum. Gazing at a picture of soldiers torturing a prisoner, he commented, "In a way, I feel more compassion for the torturers than for the victim." When asked why, he replied, "Because the suffering of the victim is over fairly quickly, but the suffering of the torturers will last a very long time."

Thinking in these ways can help us overcome negative feelings toward difficult people. We may even feel motivated to extend a helping hand to those who are troubled and needy. However, we also need to balance our compassion with wisdom. It may not always be within our capacity to benefit certain people, and trying to do so could become problematic or even harmful. In such cases, it may be wiser to keep some distance, but still have a compassionate and open-hearted attitude toward them. Simply staying calm and peaceful in their presence might be the best thing you could do. If you are open to the idea of prayer, you can pray that they receive the help they need, and that you yourself will be able to help them more in the future when the time is right. Such aspirations create the cause for our mind to become more like the minds of the buddhas and bodhisattvas, so that in the future, we will be able to benefit even the most difficult people, and cherish them like "a precious treasure."

Verse 5: Offering the Victory to Others

When others, out of jealousy,
Mistreat me with abuse, insults, and the like,
I will practice accepting defeat
And offering the victory to them.

This verse suggests a skillful way of responding when somebody wrongly blames or criticizes us, out of jealousy, or simply because she dislikes us. The usual way of reacting in such situations is to become defensive and retaliate, often with anger, but here we are advised to patiently accept what is happening and let the other person have the victory. How can we develop such an attitude? Long familiarity with the methods for cultivating loving-kindness, compassion, patience, and cherishing others more than self would enable one to feel that the other person's happiness is more important than one's own, and to think, "If she derives some benefit or satisfaction from doing this, then I can put up with it. May she be happy." But those of us who are not so familiar with these methods may find our mind flooded with feelings of hurt, anger, and the wish to strike back. If this happens, we can examine why we feel this way: why do we feel hurt and angry when someone says bad things about us? Why are we so concerned about what other people think and say? If others dislike and criticize us, does that necessarily mean we're bad? Alternatively, if others like and respect us, does that necessarily mean we're good? There's a story in the Tibetan tradition about a man who was liked and respected by everyone in his community, and as a result he came to feel that he was quite a wonderful person. But just before he died, he realized with dismay that all the respect and praise he had received had made him blind to his faults, so he had neglected to work on his spiritual development.

It can be useful, therefore, to pay attention to criticism directed at us, because we may be able to learn something from it. One of my teachers, Geshe Doga, said that there is never any reason for us to get upset if we are criticized. We should look inside ourselves and check whether the criticism is true or not. If it isn't true, the other person's words are like empty, meaningless noise, and there is no need to get upset about them. But if we check and find that the criticism *is* true, we can gratefully accept it as helpful advice for our spiritual development. It's often difficult to see ourselves objectively. We tend to be blind to our faults and mistakes, so we sometimes need others to point them out for us.

We may also get upset when we are criticized because we want to always be right, to always be the winner in any argument or conflict. It may be useful to ask, "Why is winning so important to me? And what does it mean to 'win'?" If you fight and win an argument in such a way that the other person is left feeling humiliated or bitter, will you really feel good about yourself? Have you achieved something you're satisfied with? And are things really so black and white that there is necessarily a winner and a loser in every conflict? Could it be that "winning" and "losing" are relative, just ideas or concepts in your mind, depending on how you interpret a situation, depending on what you want and expect from the situation? If you have a clear idea as to what you really want to achieve, it may be possible to settle a problem between yourself and another person in such a way that both of you come away feeling you have won.

We can also generate compassion for the person who is criticizing us by understanding that she is probably in a very disturbed state of mind, and not at all peaceful or contented. We can reflect: "It is because of anger and jealousy in her mind that she is saying these things. Such emotions are very unpleasant and disturbing, so it is impossible to be happy while they are in the mind. Also, she is not really in control of what she is doing; she is controlled by her delusions. As a result, she is suffering now, and will also suffer in the future when she has to experience the karmic results of her present actions." If we can look at the situation in this way, it will be easier to feel compassion and not wish to give harm.

All this does not mean that we should never defend ourselves when wrongly accused or blamed. The Dalai Lama says that in situations where we are obsessed with merely our own welfare, we should accept defeat and give the victory to others, but in situations where the welfare of others is at stake, then we need to work hard and fight for their rights. So there may be times when it is appropriate for us to speak up and clear false accusations or rumors, but we should do so without anger, without the wish to take revenge. Nor does it mean that we should avoid communicating with someone who is angry with us. If the person is open to communication and we are able to speak calmly and without anger, it may be possible to work out a solution to the problem that we are both happy with. What is being stressed in this verse is that we should avoid acting or speaking out of anger, bitterness, and so forth, or harboring negative thoughts in our mind toward those who harm us.

Feeling hurt and angry when criticized usually happens because we are attached to our reputation—we want others to like and respect us. According to the Tibetan masters, this is one of the most difficult attachments to let go of. There is a story about Geshe Langri Tangpa, the author of *The Eight Verses of Thought Transformation*, that illustrates how a spiritually mature person is free from such concerns. Once, a woman who had given birth to a sickly child was told by an astrologer that in order to save the child's life, she must take it to a spiritual master and claim it was his. So she brought the child to Langri Tangpa, who happened to be in the middle of giving a Dharma discourse to a large number of disciples, and put the baby on his lap saying, "This is yours." The Geshe happily accepted the infant and said, "For all my lives you have been my child." Seeing this, half of the disciples lost faith in their teacher and walked out. But Langri Tangpa continued to teach. At the end of the discourse, the mother presented the Geshe with offerings and apologized for what she had done, explaining that she did it to save the child's life. Langri Tangpa calmly handed back the child, and the disciples who had not walked out felt even greater faith in their master, seeing that he had no concern with being the victor.

Verse 6: Learning From Those Who Harm Us

> *Even if someone I have benefited*
> *And in whom I have placed great hopes*

Hurts me very badly,
I will practice seeing that one as my sublime teacher.

The situation described in this verse is more difficult to deal with than those described in the previous verses. This is because the person involved here is someone we are close to. It could be a friend, a family member, or a student, someone we have helped, and whom we expect to treat us with consideration and kindness. Instead, this person betrays our trust and hurts us in some way. The pain we experience is far greater than the pain we experience when we are hurt by someone we're not so close to. Because of our hurt and pain, we would most likely feel angry and bitter, and may even have thoughts of harming this person in return. However, this verse advises us to practice seeing that one as our sublime teacher. How can we manage to do that?

First of all, we can examine the feelings of love and caring that we had for the person. Was our love pure and unconditional, asking nothing in return, or was it conditional, tied up with expectations? Much of the time, we place expectations on our friends and loved ones. In exchange for the love, friendship, care, and help we give to them, we feel they should reciprocate by being nice to us, doing what we want them to do, and not doing what we don't want them to do. In this way, our relationships are like business contracts, with a whole set of unwritten rules such as "I'll do this for you, provided you do that for me; I will be nice to you as long as you are nice to me; I will help you as long as you do what I want." This kind of love is called "conditional love"—love with strings attached—and is not real love. Real love is unconditional. It's a sincere, heartfelt caring about the other person, with respect and acceptance of that one just as he is, without demanding or expecting anything in return.

It's dangerous to have expectations of people, because they don't always live up to our expectations; they don't always act the way we want them to. In some cases this may be deliberate—they may truly intend to hurt us—but in most cases, they're simply being themselves, doing what they want to do. If this happens to go against what we want them to do, we feel hurt, disappointed, and even angry.

The real problem is not so much what the other person did or did not do, but rather the expectations we placed on him. We need to check if our expectations were reasonable and realistic: "What did I expect of him? Was I being realistic and fair, or was I expecting too much? Would it be right for me to stop caring about this person simply because he didn't live up to my expectations?"

And now we can see why such a person is a valuable teacher. He has given us the opportunity to recognize the limits of our love. We discover that our love was not free from conditions, and was not strong enough to withstand hurt and betrayal. We may then decide that we need to work harder at developing pure, unconditional love. Therefore, if we find ourselves in the situation described here, it's useful to regard the situation as a valuable lesson, and to regard the harm-giver as a teacher. He has given us the opportunity to understand ourselves better, to see our limitations and to become aware of the areas we need to work on to perfect our love. In fact, that person is a *sublime* teacher, because it is only through facing difficulties such as this that we can develop real love, compassion, patience, and wisdom, and progress along the spiritual path.

You may argue, "But his intention was not to teach me or help me. His intention was to hurt me." That may not be the case; maybe he was just being himself, doing what *he* wanted to do. But even if he did wish to hurt you, you can attribute that to delusions in his mind and remember that these are transitory; his real nature is clear and pure. Moreover, as we saw in the meditation on the kindness of others, it's not necessary for someone to *intend* to help us for us to receive help from them. If we learn something important from a person or an experience, even a painful one, then it becomes helpful for us, even if there was no such intention involved. It's all a matter of how we choose to look at things.

Verse 7: The Practice of Taking and Giving

In short, I will offer directly and indirectly
Every benefit and happiness to all beings, my mothers.
I will practice in secret taking upon myself
All their harmful actions and sufferings.

This verse describes the practice of "taking and giving," or *tong-len* in Tibetan. This is a very powerful meditation technique used by those who are following the bodhisattva path to strengthen their love and compassion and to awaken the mind of enlightenment. It involves imagining that one is *taking* on the suffering of others, and *giving* to them one's own happiness and virtue. As we have discussed, our deep-seated me-first attitude needs to be reversed if we are to reach enlightenment. The practice of taking and giving is a very effective way gradually to overcome self-cherishing and to develop its opposite: the mind that cherishes others.

When we do this practice of taking and giving, the "taking" usually comes first. This is because it's difficult for people to be truly happy while they are suffering. A person who is very ill, for example, would find it hard to enjoy the things that normally give him pleasure until he regains his health. Therefore, we need to first remove others' sufferings, and then give them happiness. We begin by meditating on the various sufferings that others are undergoing, such as sickness and pain, aging and dying, depression, failure, dissatisfaction, fear, grief, and so on, and generate a strong, compassionate wish that all beings be free of these sufferings. We then go a step further and feel the wish to actually take their suffering upon ourselves. With this compassionate thought, we visualize all the sufferings in the form of black smoke and imagine drawing the smoke into our heart. At our heart, we visualize our self-cherishing attitude in the form of a black stone or spot. When the black smoke of others' suffering is drawn into this black spot at our heart, the spot becomes smaller and smaller until it finally disappears. At that point we feel joyful, thinking that all beings have been freed from their suffering, and our own self-cherishing attitude has been overcome.

Initially, it may be difficult to sincerely wish to take on all the sufferings of others. We may feel, "I can't even handle my own problems, so how can I take on those of others?" Because of this, we usually start the practice of taking and giving by taking on our own present and future suffering. The procedure is the same as above, but instead of focusing on the sufferings of other beings, we focus on whatever problems and difficulties we're now facing in our life. We visualize taking all these problems into our heart and imagine that doing so diminishes and destroys our selfishness. Then we think of those we can expect to face in the future—such as sickness, loss, conflict with others, frustration and disappointment, growing old and eventually dying—and visualize in the same way. Once we feel comfortable about accepting and transforming our own suffering, we can move on to imagining taking on the suffering of people with whom we are close, such as parents, relatives, and friends. Eventually, we will be able to take on the suffering of strangers and even of those we dislike.

There is a simple way of practicing "taking" that can be used whenever you experience any kind of problem. Normally you feel aversion to any unpleasant experience, and wish it to disappear as quickly as possible. You may also get caught up in self-pity, and feel as though you're the only person in the world who is suffering. This is just adding more problems to what is already there, and creating a lot of tension in your mind. Instead of this, you can use the problem to open your heart and cultivate compassion. Start by thinking: "I'm not the only one who has such a problem. There are many other people, many other beings, who are experiencing the same problem—in some cases, even worse than mine." Reflect on that for some time, thinking of specific examples. Then think, "How wonderful it would be if all those other people and beings could be free from this suffering." Really *feel* that compassionate wish. Next, decide to accept your own problem on behalf of all those other beings: "I accept this problem, this suffering, and by my accepting it, may all those other beings be relieved of theirs." This method works like magic—it brings peace and spaciousness to our mind, lightens our suffering, and expands our compassion for others.

If you find it hard to understand the wish to take on others' suffering, think of how parents feel when they see their children in pain. Parents have so much love and concern for their children that they cannot bear to see them suffer. They may even feel, "I wish I could take away my child's suffering. I would rather experience it myself than have my child suffer!" When a mother or father has this kind of love, they would willingly sacrifice their own well-being in order to take on their child's suffering and give the child their happiness in exchange. This shows that where there is strong love and compassion, people are able to generate the kind of selfless attitude expressed in this verse. We all have the potential to develop universal love and compassion, and we can all develop the sincere wish to take on the suffering of others and to give them our happiness.

After we have visualized freeing all beings from their sufferings by taking those sufferings onto ourselves and thereby destroying our self-cherishing attitude, we turn to "giving." For our practice of "giving" to be powerful, we need first to meditate on loving-kindness, the wish for all beings to have happiness and the causes of happiness, just as we discussed in chapter 2. We meditate on loving-kindness until we feel this so strongly that we wish to give our own happiness to others.

The actual meditation on giving involves visualizing all the good things we have—our happiness, good qualities, wisdom, and accumulation of virtue—in the form of light. We then imagine sending this light out to others and when it reaches them, it transforms into whatever they need in order to be happy: food for those who are hungry, money for those who are poor, medicine for those who are sick, friends for those who are lonely, spiritual encouragement for those who are doubtful, and so forth. Since everyone needs Dharma in order to attain the highest, most perfect happiness of enlightenment, we also imagine the light transforming into Dharma teachings and visualize that by receiving these, the beings attain all the realizations of the path up to enlightenment. Then we meditate on a feeling of great joy, thinking that all beings are now fully satisfied and perfectly happy.

You may wonder why the verse says, "all beings, my *mothers*." This refers to the idea that each and every living being has been our mother—not in this present lifetime, of course, but in our previous lifetimes, which are said to be countless and without beginning. In fact, as noted in chapter 7, we have been in every possible type of relationship with every living being, but that of mother and child is emphasized because, generally, our mother is more important and more kind to us than anyone else. As we discussed in the chapter on loving-kindness and in the meditation on the kindness of others, a mother is one of the best examples of unconditional love we have. She brings us into the world, feeds us, nurtures us with love and affection, protects us from harm, teaches us basic skills like walking and talking, and so on. Once we realize the vast kindness of our mother, and think of all beings as having been mother to us, we will feel closer to them, and will want to repay their kindness by helping them as much as we can. (As we said earlier, if you have a great deal of difficulty with your mother, you needn't let that be a hang-up in these meditations. You can think of other people who have shown you loving-kindness in order to get a sense of warm-heartedness.) When we are more familiar with the practice of taking and giving, we can combine it with our breathing: as we breathe in we imagine taking in others' suffering, and as we breathe out we send our happiness to others. This is an advanced level of practice, and a way to create immense merit and get closer to enlightenment with every breath.

The verse mentions doing the practice "in secret." The Dalai Lama explains this to mean that the practice of taking and giving may not be suitable for beginners, but is intended for those whose compassion is strong and well-developed. Another meaning is that the practice should not be done in a showy way, as if we want everyone to know how compassionate and selfless we are. A genuine practitioner makes profound changes in his or her mind, but remains ordinary-looking on the outside.

You may wonder whether doing this practice will actually cause you to receive someone else's sickness or actually give happiness to someone who isn't happy. That's very unlikely. According to the law of cause and effect, or karma, each of us is responsible for our own actions, and thus for our own suffering and happiness. No one can take away another person's negative karma and suffering, or give them one's own good karma and happiness. If it were possible to do so, the Buddha would have removed all our suffering and given us the perfect peace of enlightenment long ago. Taking and giving is practiced to train our own mind: to develop compassion and loving-kindness, and to overcome the self-cherishing attitude. By developing our mind in this way, eventually we will achieve enlightenment and will possess unlimited resources with which to help and guide others to freedom from suffering and its causes. Nonetheless, by practicing taking and giving with sincere compassion and love, we may be able to provide some relief to those who are suffering, and help them to feel more calm and peaceful.

Verse 8: The Illusory Nature of Phenomena

> *May all these practices be undefiled by the stains*
> *Of the eight worldly concerns,*
> *And by perceiving all phenomena as illusory,*
> *May I be released from the bondage of attachment.*

There are two very important Buddhist teachings contained in this verse. The first is the need to keep our Dharma practice pure, free of the eight worldly concerns. The second is the understanding of the real nature of all phenomena—that they are like illusions. Understanding the illusory nature of all phenomena will free us from disturbing emotions such as attachment so that we can then help others likewise to become free.

What are the eight worldly concerns? They are concern about gain and loss, pleasant and unpleasant experiences, praise and blame, and reputation or lack of it. We feel happy when we receive or possess things, unhappy when we lose or are unable to get what we desire; happy when we have pleasant experiences, unhappy when we experience anything unpleasant; happy when someone praises us, unhappy when we are blamed or criticized; happy when our reputation is good, unhappy when our reputation is bad or we are unknown.

These eight concerns can be condensed into two attitudes: being attached to what is pleasant, and having aversion or fear toward whatever is unpleasant. Whenever we encounter or obtain something pleasant, our mind feels happy and excited, and becomes attached to whatever brought us that pleasure. On the other hand, whenever we encounter someone or something unpleasant, ugly, frightening, or uncomfortable, our mind feels unhappy, irritated, or angry, and develops aversion toward that object.

As we touched on when discussing the fifth verse, one of the best examples of our reactivity is praise and criticism. When people point out our good qualities, or tell us that we have done something really well, our mind goes up and we feel elated and excited. But whenever we face the opposite—criticism, blame, or unkind words—our mind goes down and we feel depressed, unhappy, and negative. We may even become angry and want to hurt the person who criticized us.

Gain and loss is another major concern. When someone gives us a gift, when we go shopping and buy ourselves new clothes or gadgets, or when we get a raise in salary, we feel happy and become attached to the object or to the person who gave it. But when we do not get what we want, or when we lose something that we cherish, our mind goes down and we become unhappy, depressed, and angry.

This is what the eight worldly concerns are all about: being overly concerned about the good and bad things that happen in our life. One problem with this is that if we allow our mind to be influenced by these attitudes, they will leave us at the mercy of conditions over which we have no control, such as what people think and say about us, or whether we encounter pleasant or unpleasant experiences. As a result, our mind goes up and down like a yo-yo—one moment happy, the next moment unhappy; one moment full of love and kindness, the next full of anger and resentment. They cause our mind to be uptight and fearful; we are afraid of losing the things we are attached to, and of meeting what we do not like. These eight attitudes also tend to be self-centered—they are concerned about getting what *I* like and avoiding what *I* don't like—and thus are an obstacle to developing genuine concern for others. They get us caught up in experiences and objects that are impermanent, and that we will have to leave behind when we journey to the next life. Furthermore, under their influence, we may act unwisely, such as behaving pretentiously in order to win others' attention and praise, or stealing things we desire but cannot afford to buy. The eight worldly concerns are thus a source of problems in this life and an obstacle to future happiness and spiritual development.

Is it wrong, then, to experience pleasure and to not want pain? That's not what is being said here. There is nothing wrong with pleasant experiences, relationships, a good reputation, money, or material possessions. The problem is being *attached* to these things. And we learned about all the problems of attachment in chapter 2. Remember: what we truly want is happiness, but attachment is actually an obstacle to that. It makes our mind disturbed and tense, such that we are unable to just relax and enjoy things. And we *can* enjoy pleasant experiences without selfish attachment. One way of doing this, which also increases our love and compassion, is to mentally share the experience with all other beings, by thinking, for example, "May all beings have plenty of healthy, delicious food like this," or "I wish all beings could be here in this peaceful place, watching this beautiful sunset."

We need to be especially alert to the eight worldly concerns influencing our practice of Dharma. For example, we may want people to be impressed by how much we know about Dharma, by our patience or our diligence in practice, by the amount of money we donate to a charitable cause or the amount of time we spend doing social work. We hope others will notice how long we are able to sit in meditation with our back perfectly straight, looking serene and sublime like the Buddha. We are full of enthusiasm when our practice is going well, but when we encounter problems we become depressed and discouraged, and think about giving it up. These are signs that the eight worldly concerns have crept into our Dharma practice. When this happens, it means that our practice has become polluted or "defiled," and is actually the cause of further confusion and suffering rather than of peace, happiness, and spiritual growth.

What should we do if we notice any of these eight attitudes in our mind? First, we should try to avoid being upset with ourselves, thinking, "Oh, I'm so bad; I'm such a lousy practitioner!" Instead we should be happy that we have become aware of a problem that we have always had but never noticed before. Now we can do something about it.

The best remedy to the eight worldly concerns is to reflect once again on impermanence: the changing nature of all things, one of the antidotes we discussed in chapter 1. The pleasant and unpleasant events and experiences of this life are not permanent—they last only a short time and then disappear. It's unwise, then, to cling to what is pleasant, wishing it to last forever, or to be upset by what is unpleasant, since it will soon vanish. Furthermore, our very life is impermanent: we are going to die one day and when we do, everything in this life—relationships, possessions, pleasant and unpleasant memories, reputation, and so on—will fade and disappear like last night's dream.

The second teaching contained in this verse is that all phenomena are like illusions. This refers to the Buddha's teaching on emptiness, also known as "selflessness." Emptiness is the actual, correct way in which everything exists: oneself, all other people and living beings, all inanimate phenomena. It is the ultimate, true nature of all things. Emptiness is not somewhere far away or up in space. We don't have to travel to a place like the Himalayas to find it. Emptiness is right here, right now. It is the true nature of our body and mind, our thoughts and feelings, and everyone and everything around us.

Emptiness is not nothingness. It doesn't mean that things do not exist at all. Things *do* exist, but they do not exist the way we think they do. Our mind projects a way of existing onto the objects we perceive—like an extra layer on top of what is actually there—and then we believe that they really do exist that way. However, although things exist, they are *empty* of the false, mistaken way of existing that our mind projects onto them. That false way of existing is called "inherent existence," "independent existence," or "true existence." It means that we see things as if they were permanent, independent, existing from their own side, in and of themselves. If we carefully analyze, we will come to see that things do not exist in this way—that such a way of existing is false, an illusion.

Incidentally, the phrase "existing from its own side" is often used in discussions of emptiness. While it is not everyday English usage, it is a helpful phrase to point out that we break things down into subject (our side, this side) and object (its own side, the other side). Then, we imagine that something could exist "from its own side," with no relationship to "our side." If we contemplate matters closely, we will come to see that the relationship between "this side" and the "other side" is interdependent. Nothing exists independently, from its own side.

Take a flower, for example. When we walk into a room and see a flower in a vase, we instinctively perceive the flower as something permanent, unchanging, existing all on its own, from its own side, as if it did not depend on anything else for its existence. It seems very real, concrete, out there, existing in and of itself—almost as if it jumps out to meet us saying, "I'm a flower. I've always been here and always will be here, just like this!" This is how the flower appears to us and we believe it to exist in this way. But this way of appearing and the actual way the flower exists are quite different. In reality the flower is impermanent, is dependent on various causes and conditions, and does not exist in and of itself. The flower came into existence in dependence upon a seed, soil, moisture, and sunlight. It grew little by little and when it was in full bloom, someone cut it and placed it in a vase. Its existence is also dependent on its parts: stem, petals, stamen, as well as on the cells and atoms that make it up. When first cut, the flower is fresh and beautiful but as the days go by, it withers and turns brown, and soon it will die and be thrown into the rubbish. That is the true story of the flower, but that is not what we see when we look at it. When we look at it, it seems to be unchanging and autonomous, independent of anything else.

On top of that, our mind grasps at the object being a flower from its own side, not realizing that "flower" is just a name or label that people have given to a collection of parts—none of which is a flower—that has certain characteristics, not realizing that people of other languages would call it by other names and various animals would perceive it altogether differently according to their sensory world. So, although there appears to be a real, solid, permanent, and independently existing flower out there, when we investigate and search for such a flower, it cannot be found. Such a flower is an illusion—like a dream or a rainbow. It appears, but does not exist the way it appears. But this does not mean that there is no flower at all. Conventionally, there *is* a flower—there is an impermanent collection of parts that came into existence in dependence on causes and conditions, goes through changes, and will go out of existence, and to which we give the name "flower." *That* exists, but not the permanent, independently existing flower that we perceive and grasp at when we say, "Oh, isn't it beautiful!"

In the same way, all things appear to be inherently and independently existent, but on closer examination, we realize that they exist in a completely different way. And that is their reality, their true nature: being empty of inherent existence.

"So what?" you may wonder. "Why should I be concerned about this?" We should be concerned because this tendency to perceive, believe in, and grasp at things as truly existing or inherently existing lies at the root of all our problems. Fear, worry, frustration, dissatisfaction, loneliness, grief, pain, and all the other myriad problems and sufferings of mind and body we experience are caused by this attitude, which in Buddhism is known as "self-grasping ignorance." We all have the potential to enjoy ever-lasting peace and freedom—the state of enlightenment or Buddhahood—but we are unable to attain this as long as our mind is caught up in ignorance, and does not understand the true nature of things.

Self-grasping ignorance pervades our view of everything. We see ourselves as inherently existing—we cling tightly to an illusory image of a permanent, independently existing I or self. We hold on to self-limiting concepts about ourselves, believing that mistakes made in the past have become permanent aspects of our personality. These "permanent faults" become the basis of low self-esteem and even self-hatred, obscuring our potential to be pure, perfect, and free—an enlightened being. All this arises from ignorant misperception.

Moreover, we tend to cherish our sense of self, as if it were the center of the universe. Out of this strong self-centeredness, which we've discussed at length in this book, we develop desire and attachment for people and things that make us happy and support our sense of I, we have aversion and fear toward people and things that disturb us or threaten our sense of I, and we are indifferent toward whoever or whatever neither helps nor harms us. We are now looking directly at the root cause of our self-centeredness. Believing all people and objects to exist in a real, permanent, independent way intensifies our attitudes of attachment and aversion. These attitudes disturb our mind and motivate us to create negative actions or karma, such as harming our enemies, and lying or stealing to benefit ourselves and our loved ones, and this karma is the cause of suffering and problems in the future. Self-grasping ignorance is also the main factor that keeps us circling in samsara, the wheel of death and rebirth.

That is why we should be concerned about our tendency to see things as truly or inherently existent, and why we should learn to perceive things in their correct way, as empty of inherent existence, or, as it says in the verse, as "illusory." A simple way to understand this is by thinking of the analogy of a rainbow. Due to certain conditions in the atmosphere and the play of sunlight and moisture, a rainbow appears in the sky. Although it looks so real we would like to touch it, it is insubstantial, momentary, and completely dependent on causes and conditions. It exists for a while and then disappears. Everything else, all phenomena—animate and inanimate—are like the rainbow. Although most things last longer than a rainbow, the way they exist is similar: they do not exist substantially or independently, but depend on various factors such as causes, conditions, parts, and mental labeling. So, like a rainbow, they are illusory, empty of independent, substantial existence.

Keeping in mind that all things are illusory, a bodhisattva engages in the practice of Dharma, the path leading to enlightenment, without grasping at anyone or anything as truly existing. In this way the bodhisattva frees him- or herself from disturbing states of mind and karma—the causes of all suffering in the prison of samsara—and works to help all other living beings to likewise become free.

I chose to explain the *Eight Verses* to show the relevance of this precious little text, from another time and another culture, to our lives in this present time. In my own experience I've found these verses to be extremely helpful. They teach us different ways of looking at and dealing with challenging situations, so that in place of feeling disturbed and unhappy, we can remain calm, clear, and compassionate. Practicing them takes courage and strength, but if we are able to do so, we will be able to grow tremendously in wisdom and unselfishness. I'm certain that, deep down in our hearts, that is what we all long for. The *Eight Verses* make an excellent complement to the four immeasurables and the meditations and antidotes associated with those four sublime thoughts.

The Buddha attained the perfect peace of enlightenment long ago, but our minds are still confused and disturbed, and we are still trapped in the cycle of birth, death, and suffering. The Buddha gave up his self-cherishing attitude long ago, whereas we are still very much attached to ours. We too can achieve what the Buddha achieved, but we must work on ourselves—putting effort into changing our mind, our attitudes. We need to learn to be less self-centered, more concerned for others; less angry, more patient; less grasping, more detached; less unkind, more compassionate.

As I have said so often here, you *can* change, provided you are willing to train in practices like those explained in the thought transformation teachings and in the four immeasurables. But, remember, it takes time to change the mind. It is not something that you can expect to happen in a few months or even in a few years. Be patient and compassionate toward yourself. Compassionately accept yourself as you are now, while knowing that it's possible to change. Steadily put your energy into practices that will enable changes to take place, that will enable the clouds to part from the clear, blue sky of your mind so that your naturally existing kind heart may awaken.

Notes

1   *The Dalai Lama, A Policy of Kindness*, compiled and edited by Sidney Piburn (Ithaca, New York: Snow Lion Publications, 1990), p. 52.

2   For more information on this text, its background, and its author, see Geshe Tsultrim Gyeltsen, *Keys to Enlightenment* (Los Angeles: Thubten Dhargyey Ling Publications, 1989), pp. 47–50.

3   From the foreword by His Holiness the Fourteenth Dalai Lama to *Training the Mind in the Great Way* by Gyalwa Gendun Druppa, the First Dalai Lama, translated by Glenn H. Mullin (Ithaca, New York: Snow Lion Publications, 1993), p. 12.

4   *The Guru Puja* (Dharmasala: Library of Tibetan Works and Archives, 1979), p. 43.

5   A practice composed by Lama Zopa Rinpoche, which combines visualization and prayer to Avalokitesvara with meditation on the *Eight Verses*, can be found in *How to Meditate* by Kathleen McDonald (Boston: Wisdom Publications, 1984), pp. 160–170.

Other Books About Loving-Kindness, Compassion, and Thought Transformation

Chodron, Pema. *Start Where You Are*. Boston: Shambala Publications, 1994.

Chodron, Thubten. *Open Heart, Clear Mind*. Ithaca, New York: Snow Lion Publications, 1991.

Dalai Lama, The. *The Compassionate Life*. Boston: Wisdom Publications, 2003.

Dalai Lama, His Holiness the. *Transforming the Mind*. London: Thorsons, 2000.

Gyalwa Gendun Druppa, the First Dalai Lama. *Training the Mind in the Great Way*. Translated by Glenn H. Mullin. Ithaca, New York: Snow Lion Publications, 1993.

Hopkins, Jeffrey. *A Truthful Heart*. Ithaca, New York: Snow Lion Publications, 2008.

Kongtrul, Jamgon. *The Great Path of Awakening*. Translated by Ken McLeod. Boston: Shambala Publications, 1987.

Rabten, Geshe and Geshe Ngawang Dhargyey. *Advice from a Spiritual Friend*. Boston: Wisdom Publications, 1996.

Rinchen, Geshe Sonam. *Eight Verses for Training the Mind*. Ithaca, New York: Snow Lion Publications, 2001.

Salzburg, Sharon. *Lovingkindness—the Revolutionary Art of Happiness*. Boston: Shambala Publications, 1995

Shantideva. *The Way of the Bodhisattva*. Boston: Shambala Publications, 1997.

Wallace, Alan B. *The Four Immeasurables: Cultivating a Boundless Heart*. Ithaca, New York: Snow Lion Publications: 2004

Wangchen, Geshe Namgyal. *Step By Step: Basic Buddhist Meditations*. Boston: Wisdom Publications, 2009.

Zopa Rinpoche, Lama. *How to be Happy*. Edited by Josh Bartok and Ailsa Cameron. Boston: Wisdom Publications, 2008.

Zopa Rinpoche, Lama. *Transforming Problems into Happiness*. Edited by Ailsa Cameron and Robina Courtin. Boston: Wisdom Publications, 1993.

About the Author

KATHLEEN MCDONALD (Sangye Khadro) was ordained as a Tibetan Buddhist nun in 1974. She is a respected and inspiring teacher in the Foundation for the Preservation of the Mahayana Tradition (FPMT), a worldwide organization of Buddhist centers, medical clinics, and schools. She is the author of the bestselling *How to Meditate* and the coauthor, with Lama Zopa Rinpoche, of *Wholesome Fear*.

About Wisdom Publications

WISDOM PUBLICATIONS, a nonprofit publisher, is dedicated to making available authentic works relating to Buddhism for the benefit of all. We publish books by ancient and modern masters in all traditions of Buddhism, translations of important texts, and original scholarship. Additionally, we offer books that explore East-West themes unfolding as traditional Buddhism encounters our modern culture in all its aspects. Our titles are published with the appreciation of Buddhism as a living philosophy, and with the special commitment to preserve and transmit important works from Buddhism's many traditions.

To learn more about Wisdom, or to browse books online, visit our website at www.wisdompubs.org.

You may request a copy of our catalog online or by writing to this address:

Wisdom Publications
199 Elm Street
Somerville, Massachusetts 02144 USA
Telephone: 617-776-7416
Fax: 617-776-7841
Email: info@wisdompubs.org
www.wisdompubs.org

The Wisdom Trust

As a nonprofit publisher, Wisdom is dedicated to the publication of Dharma books for the benefit of all sentient beings and dependent upon the kindness and generosity of sponsors in order to do so. If you would like to make a donation to Wisdom, you may do so through our website or our Somerville office. If you would like to help sponsor the publication of a book, please write or email us at the address above.

Thank you.

Wisdom is a nonprofit, charitable 501(c)(3) organization affiliated with the Foundation for the Preservation of the Mahayana Tradition (FPMT).